EMOTIONAL ⌣⎽⎽⎽⎽

EMOTIONAL SELLING

Using Emotional Intelligence to Get Sales

David Yule

2000

Published in 2000 by Management Books 2000 Ltd
Cowcombe House,
Cowcombe Hill,
Chalford,
Gloucestershire GL6 8HP
Tel. 01285-760722 Fax: 01285-760708
e-mail: MB2000@compuserve.com

Printed and bound in Great Britain by Biddles, Guildford

British Library Cataloguing in Publication Data is available

ISBN 1-85252-314-X

Acknowledgements

I would like to acknowledge the people who have had an influence on me and my selling and consequently this book.

Most of all, my wife Julie. Otherwise they are in no particular order and I am sorry if I have left anyone out who feels they should be included.

Pat McAvoy, Chris Howe, Simon Percival, Steve Wood, Mark Walton, Owen Reed, Nick Brice, Avril Carson, John Elder, Goran Gorrson, David Hall, Martin Humphries, Chris Lane, Norman Longdon, Sue Moore, Carole Neales, Sonia & Richard Nelson, Mike Pegg, George Schaphoff, Larry Winget, Peter Thompson, Eric Nicoli, Lucy Caldwell, Mike Wilson, Robert Gravill, James Retallack, Andy Bain, Billy, George and James (my brothers).

To Julie, Mum, Inga and Lindsay

Contents

1

Introduction

Most buying decisions are based on emotional logic. It has been estimated that over 80 per cent of all decisions are based on emotion. We have all been in situations where logically the customer should have bought our product and yet they didn't buy it. That is because customers don't have to follow the rules. Every selling process I have encountered has been based on logical reasons. It is very easy to see how, logically, they work. There is no 100 per cent guaranteed sales process because selling is not a perfect science. There are no right or wrong ways to do it. I use the psychological needs of the customer to appeal to their emotions and increase my chance of getting a sale.

In the entire world there are only 3 ways to increase your sales. The three ways are:

- Increase Your Number Of Customers
- Increase Your Average Order Value
- Increase The Frequency of Orders

My intention is to work on all three ways to give as many practical tips as possible. The entire focus is tactical rather than strategic selling. What you can do differently when you are in front of the customer to get more sales. My overriding rule for selling is that if you aren't having fun you are probably doing it wrongly and so I will have some fun in the book as well.

I know the practical tools in this book do work. How do I know they work? Well, I was in the fortunate (??) position for nearly ten years of having a role which mainly concerned sales coaching. This meant I was able to observe the methods we used to train salespeople and check out whether they really worked in practice. I discovered that many of the things that were considered to be necessary to sell well don't work in practice. I don't think you will ever meet someone who has the same view towards selling as me. If you want to know why I say the following examples of good selling techniques are mistakes, then you will need to read on!

Some of the conventions in selling that don't stand up to practical examination may be familiar:-

- **People buy from people they like.**
  In fact they buy from people they *trust* and that is a very different thing from liking. That is why modern selling does not have 'The 7 Steps of Successful Selling' or anything like it. Selling is about *building trust.*

- **Salespeople treat people as individuals.**
  It is strange how many salespeople don't treat everyone differently. Wouldn't you like to know more about customers? Which are more loyal, which are less price sensitive and which are low 'shoppers'? Read about them in Chapter 4 – Deal with the Behaviour!

- **The salesperson just has to ask the customer/client what they want.**
  In my experience most customers don't know what they want, they don't know what they need, and what they want and what they need are two different things! See Chapter 7 – Finding Out What People Really, REALLY Want.

- **Customers are more knowledgeable today than they have ever been.**
  They may be more streetwise, they know how to play the buying/selling game, but... they are certainly not more knowledgeable about products.
  Products are so complex now and there is so much choice it is impossible to be more knowledgeable. Insurance is a good example of this. A simple subject with only three options:

Option 1 If you die within a given period the insurance pays.
Option 2 Whenever you die the insurance pays. Or:
Option 3 If you survive a given period the insurance pays.

It isn't complicated enough! So to differentiate themselves in the market place insurance companies dress up these simple concepts as complex products with much small print and brand names dreamt up by marketers. They design something that needs the advice or help of a salesperson.

- **Salespeople make it simple for customers.**
  I should certainly like a simple – preferably small – telephone bill instead of a package where I first have to decide who are my Top 10 best friends, or whether I should take x 'free' minutes or go for the discount service item of the month? Which car purchase package to go for, the one with 0% finance and a hefty residual payment, or the one with the three year, unlimited mileage warranty? And who can figure out the cheapest deal between three competing junk mail credit card issuers? Products and the differences between them are so complex now it is really impossible for consumers to be more knowledgeable. Streetwise yes ('If I were you, I wouldn't have bought one of those...'), knowledgeable no. Consumer 'choice' is fast becoming an alias for total consumer confusion.

- **Salespeople who maintain a positive attitude are more successful**.
  In fact I have seen some of the most cynical people succeed in selling. and if someone convinced them it was a great product or solution then it had to be good.

  In this world there seems to be any number of people who will tell you all you have to do is forecast some earnings figure you would like to make and then somehow magically you will achieve it. Like Del Boy – 'This time next year, Rodney, we'll be millionaires'. I think people become millionaires by focusing their efforts on what they are doing today, not dreaming about tomorrow. Also, some psychologists (Larkin, McDermott, Simon & Simon 1980) discovered that to solve a problem experts work

forwards towards a solution, whereas novices work backwards...
It is a novice solution to 'start with the end in mind'. Start out with
having no money and a strategy to get some today!

- **There are some things in selling you must never do!**
  If this is correct then the list must be very small. I have seen
  salespeople doing the weirdest things. If you do anything in the
  right spirit with the right tone, etc., most things are acceptable.
  (One top salesman for a radio station was collecting performance
  bonuses, until he was had up for demanding money with
  menaces!)

- **Successful salespeople have an outstanding knowledge of
  competitor products.**
  Absolutely not! This simply leads to the salesperson trying to
  attack the competitor product, (sometimes subtly, sometimes not
  so). More knowledge seemed to influence the salesperson's
  questions. The greater the knowledge the more closed questions;
  e.g., 'Would you like something that is faster, bigger, brighter?'
  More success was gained when the competitor product was
  ignored (or even praised!). Mentioning or even attacking a
  competitor product gives it credence. I know this is controversial
  with most salespeople, it is emotional. You need to think about
  how you use competitor knowledge. If you use it to show that
  your product is better, then customers hear you 'knocking' the
  competitor product. Even asking obvious questions about their
  needs can have this effect. It is like when you say to someone,
  'You are looking really great today' and people say or think,
  'You mean I don't look great every day?' We read more into
  what is being said than what is being said and hear only what we
  want to hear.

- **People buy Benefits not Features.**
  If this were the case why do people who live in Central London
  buy 4-wheel drive, off-road vehicles? Read all about it in Chapter
  8 - Propose Solutions.

- **The more benefits a salesperson offers, the more successful they will be.**
  My research shows that in fact the success ratio can go down with more benefits. Chapter 8 – Proposing Solutions.

- **Objections are opportunities.**
  They may well be but if you can handle them before they arise you will be more successful. If you think objections are opportunities then why don't you create some at the beginning of a sale just to make sure you have some opportunities? Buying signals are whenever a customer does anything: talk, object, touch, listen, etc. People who don't buy, don't get involved. Chapter 9 – Addressing Concerns.

- **There are magic answers and shortcuts in selling.**
  Oh yes and there really is a Santa!

- **Because it is easy to understand it is easy to do.**
  Although selling is very simple it is not easy.

When 2=1

I have firm statistical evidence for the principles outlined in this book. However, you should bear in mind that almost anything can be proved "statistically". For example, if I could show you statistically how 2 is equal to 1 then you would be sceptical of any statistical evidence, wouldn't you? OK, here goes.

First of all, the laws of Mathematics state that for any equation provided you do the same to both sides of the equation then the equation is still valid (trust me, I'm a doctor!). Take the following equation:

$$a = b$$

Multiply each side by a:

$$a^2 = ab$$

Add $a^2 - 2ab$ to each side

$$a^2 + a^2 - 2ab = ab + a^2 - 2ab$$

This can be simplified to

$$2(a^2 - ab) = (a^2 - ab)$$

Divide each side by $(a^2 - ab)$ and you get:

$$2 = 1$$

It may look complicated and you may not understand algebra but I have followed all the algebraic rules. Of course there is a trick. The answer is at the end of the book (you don't have to read all the book first, evidence shows that is unlikely, turn now and find out how it's done). If you worked it out on your own you are way too smart for me (but do you sell as much as you should do, given how smart you are?).

This book has been set out so that the first section deals with external aspects; i.e., the special needs of customers and clients. The second section deals with internal actions; i.e., what I need to do in order to sell. If you want to, just skip to the second section – OK by me, but please read the entire book if you can! Every page contains something that you will find to be useful and a rationale for doing something in a certain way. Please don't trust any of it. What I have found works with the majority of people may not work for you. You cannot copy someone else's style. You must develop your own although I often hear my old boss's voice inside my head when I am selling (thanks Pat!).

What I would encourage you to do is try everything and remember it is believed that it takes 23 days to break a habit – so stick at it.

I have used the terms 'Customer' and 'Client' and 'Product' and 'Service' as being interchangeable. Having worked in the professions with their clients and services and with manufacturers and their products the techniques apply to both situations.

I hope you enjoy the book – it represents all that I knew about selling the day that I finished writing it. I have now moved on and I hope you have too through reading this.

Summary

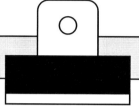

- *The only 3 ways to increase your sales are:*

  - *Increase Your Number Of Customers*
  - *Increase Your Average Order Value*
  - *Increase The Frequency of Orders*

- *You need to sell features as well as benefits (see Chapter 8 – Propose Solutions)*

- *People buy from people they trust*

- *Customers don't often know what they want or need*

- *Customers are changing and are more streetwise*

- *Some customers are loyal and some are more price sensitive find out how to identify them in Chapter 4 – Deal with the Behaviour*

- *Anything can work given the right tone and intention*

- *There are no magic answers*

- *It is not enough to have a positive attitude*

- *Salespeople need to have an outstanding knowledge of their own products.*

- *It can be a disadvantage to know too much about competitor's products.*

- *If you handle objections before they arise you will be more successful.*

NOTES:

To make things easier when a new concept is introduced it is shown in bold. This means there is a reference to the concept at the rear. The concept will then be shown in italics wherever it appears.

Reading a book about selling all the way through would be very boring. I have included my entire collection of humour that I have collected over the years from the Internet. At the end of each chapter is something I hope will amuse you.

Trust me!

ƒ

2

In the Beginning

I want to look first of all at the type of people who are increasing their skills in selling by attending training courses. It is relevant to how I recommend you should read the book. I have discovered four distinct types of people who attend training courses:

Group 1   Prisoners

They didn't want to attend the course. Someone made them do it (their boss etc.) There are 1000 things they would rather be doing than attending the course and 999 of them are probably more important than wasting their time on a training course. They are probably right!

Group 2   Holidaymakers

They didn't want to attend the course either. Someone made them do it as well and they decided to come with a different attitude. They thought 'it's better than working isn't it, and someone else is buying lunch and they would get to talk to other people in the same position so they would probably enjoy it anyway'. I am with them!

Group 3   Students

They may or may not have wanted to attend the course. Someone probably made them do it (their boss, maybe.). Their attitude is, if they have to be there, then they may as well try to get something that they can take back and use. If they can get one thing that gets them a sale then it will be worthwhile.

Of course there is always the opportunity that the course may be quite good and they will get something that is useful and they can use it everyday and get more sales all the time and then it will have been really worthwhile. They still look at everything with a critical eye. They don't take anything as gospel (that would be a disciple not a student).

I think everyone who either goes on a course or reads a book like this should adopt this attitude. Everything should be considered with a little scepticism. Try things out for yourself – don't believe everything you hear or read (even in this book) because without even trying I am obviously putting only one side of the story.

The best example of Student behaviour for me happened on a course I attended many years ago. The trainer said 'Do you know what the worst thing in retail selling is?' At this point on courses I often feel like saying 'give me a clue – how many syllables?' Anyway he said the worst thing in retail selling was when a salesperson said to a customer 'Can I help you?' This, he explained, was a closed question and as a result customers would answer 'No Thanks I'm just looking'. His answer was to ask, 'How can I help you?'

I thought this was brilliant. If I say, 'How can I help you?' then people have to answer! So the very next day I went up to a customer in the showroom and said 'How can I help you?' They obviously hadn't been on the course because they said, 'You can't thanks, we are just looking'. Another brilliant idea which is so logical and yet it doesn't work in practice because customers don't have to play the game!

Group 4   Explorers

Explorers wanted to attend the course; they may even have paid for it themselves. They come with an entirely positive attitude trying to find anything that is useful to them. They will adapt anything that works into their style. If it works for someone it can work for them.

My hope is that because you decided to read the book you are an explorer or at least a student. I am sure you will find enough to challenge you. I promise you it's simple but it's not easy and there are many benefits to trying.

The Psychology of Understanding

I also think it is necessary to look at how we learn new things. We go through a process that is known as the **Psychology of Understanding**. This has 4 stages:

- **Unconscious Incompetence**
- **Conscious Incompetence**
- **Conscious Competence**
- **Unconscious Competence**

Unconscious Incompetence

We don't know what we don't know.

For example if you ask a 16-year-old if they can drive a car the answer could be something like:

'Yes, that's the accelerator, that's the clutch, and that's the brake and my father can do it so anyone can!'

At this stage they don't know that they don't know how to drive a car.

Conscious Incompetence

We know what we don't know.

At this stage the youngster has turned seventeen, the driving licence has dropped on the doormat. They quickly say, 'Come on Dad it's my first lesson'. They jump into the car. They don't realise it yet but they start to find out that there are some things about driving that they haven't noticed.

For example they want to start the car immediately. Father says, 'Hang on! You haven't checked the gear shift is in neutral, the seating position, the wing and interior mirrors'. They haven't noticed this being done and to be fair if you are anything like me it's not too surprising they haven't noticed. It would take a very observant person to spot me doing these things! None the less they are not put off and still at this stage they think they can drive. It is only when they actually put the car into first gear that it hits them. They experience what is lovingly called 'Kangaroo Petrol' and find out that driving may be a little trickier than they thought. Anyway, they now know that they don't know how to drive.

Conscious Competence

Undaunted by this terrifying experience they practise and eventually they learn to drive. At this stage it is mostly mechanical and they have been given some triggers to help them; (e.g., Mirror – Signal – Manoeuvre is a trigger to help them remember what they should do when moving off.) They still need to think about the process of driving, processes such as: Junction – Brakes – Slowing down – Checking no other cars or worse are coming! Now they are at *Conscious Competence*.

Unconscious Competence

You don't have to think about it, you just do it.

This is the 'easy as falling off a log' stage. At this stage you have been driving for some time and you control the car automatically. In fact now you can drive an entire journey without remembering anything about it. I have said to myself many times 'were these lights at red just now?'

The difficulty with being at this stage is that if anything changes you immediately go right back to incompetence. To test this out, try driving a friend's car where the windscreen wipers are on the other side of the steering column. Or try driving an automatic car when you are used to a manual or vice versa. Be careful because when you have learned to do things automatically it is very difficult to change. The good news is you can learn both ways. I have an automatic car and my wife a manual gearbox. Both of us can jump in either car without thinking and simply drive. Riding a bike is another example of *Unconscious Competence*. Try describing how you balance a bike to a child. It's very difficult and sounds something like, 'Well, you just sort of keep it up...'

Old Chinese Proverb
(written way back in my tea break)

He who knows not and knows not he knows not is a fool – shun him

He who knows not and knows he knows not is a student – teach him

He who knows and knows he knows is wise - seek him

He who knows and knows not he knows is asleep – waken him

What is the relevance of this to selling? If you accept that if things change you will find it difficult to deal with them. How about your market place? What changes are happening? Are customers the same, loyal, nice, friendly, known commodity they were in the past or like me have you experienced a change? My customers are becoming much more knowledgeable about negotiating, some becoming more mistrusting, more demanding, and more astute. Has your competition

21

changed with more competitors, more quality products, and an ability to consistently build quality products at a lower price?

The selling process I was taught in 1980 applies today just as it did then but it works with much fewer people.

Successful selling today is about changing your style to suit the customer. I like Indian Curry, it is my favourite food but if I were to go fishing using Indian Curry as bait would I catch anything? What if the fish don't like curry? In selling, as in fishing, you must use what the customer likes rather than the salesperson. We have all had to change our style and I still see some inconsistencies. People do find it hard to leave something that was successful over many years and they don't know what or how to change.

If customers' expectations and needs, and the market place, are changing then there needs to be a change to the sales process in order to respond. For the vast majority of customers the concept that you take them through a sales process is dead and gone! We can no longer afford to go through the x steps of selling.

The Sales Process is:-

- Motivate People to Talk to You
- Help Find out Their Needs
- Propose Alternatives
- Ask for Commitment.

The order is controlled by the 'real' needs of the client. See Chapter 7 – Finding Out What People Really, REALLY Want!

You can go through the selling process in any order that is appropriate. Gone are the days that salespeople should say 'I'm sorry you can't order yet because I haven't told you about the benefits yet!' (Any future jokes I will put in italics so that you will know when to laugh).

The bad news is how difficult it is to change something you have done at an unconscious level. There is a circus act that is based on this. They challenge you to ride a bike for just 10 yards with all the controls back to front. The handlebars turn the wrong way and the pedals work backwards. It is difficult to change something you have done on an unconscious level.

We don't generally think about the construction of what we are going to say and it is this very construction of what we say that is at the heart of selling skills. I don't think about what I am going to say or how I will say it until after I have heard myself do so! This means that to change our way of communicating will be very difficult and will take some preplanning and effort and time. In any event I would be most disappointed if I had spent 20 years learning how to sell and you could pick it up easily by reading a book. (Sorry that was a joke and should have been in italics).

Have you ever met someone who continually said the same word; e.g., 'actually'? Well they don't actually say actually every actual word but actually if you actually count them you wouldn't actually believe how may times they actually say actually. In order to stop doing so they have to go through the *Psychology of Understanding* process in order to change. First of all they must recognise they do say actually a lot! (They normally need someone to point this out). Then they will hear themselves saying it just after they have said it. Later they will recognise it either during or just before saying it. Finally they will be able to have a conversation without the offending word. It won't stop there however because now they will hear everyone else saying 'actually'!! Then they will basically then substitute basically a new word, basically for themselves.

In my experience people generally are at all 4 levels of the *Psychology of Understanding* in different ways. Most people who are reading this book do something they haven't thought about and when they do think about it they want to change it (*Unconscious Incompetence*). Most people have what they consider weak spots (*Conscious Incompetence*). Most people know there are some situations they know exactly how to deal with (*Conscious Competence*). Finally, most people do many things naturally exactly as they should do without even giving it a thought (*Unconscious Competence*).

Let me give you an example, which may take you through the 4 stages. Can you imagine a ball that when you drop it, it bounces back to half the height you dropped it from? That's not too difficult is it? If it bounces half the height can you imagine that it would take half the length of time to bounce?

Then if you can imagine this you may be at *Conscious Competence*. That's good. Now this means the ball can never come to rest. If it bounces to half the distance, then if it was dropped from 8 feet it would bounce to 4 feet, then 2 feet and so on. No matter how often it bounced there is always, (at some point it would be immeasurable), but there would always be a distance for it to bounce half of. Still with me? OK, are you still at *Conscious Competence*, because I now lose myself! If the ball takes half the time to bounce the half distance it dropped it can never take longer than double the length of time of the first drop. If the first drop were 1 second the next would be ½ a second the next ¼ a second and so on but the total of these never comes to more than 2 seconds. Are you still at *Conscious Competence*? If so, you can imagine a ball that never stops bouncing and never takes longer than two seconds to do so.

Three men go into a restaurant and the bill comes to £30. They each pay £10 to the waiter who goes to put the money into the till. The manager stops him and says because they are good customers he wants to give them back £5. The waiter returns to the table and asks the diners how they would like him to divide up the £5. The men reply that because of the difficulty of dividing £5 by 3 he should give each of them one pound and keep two pounds for himself. This means that each diner has paid £9; i.e., £10 less £1. OK, if they each paid £9 then since three times nine is £27, add the £2 the waiter has and you have only £29. Where has the other £1 gone? (Don't ask me I only hear them and pass them on!)*.

I hope this chapter has given you the desire to look at new methods and consider working hard in order to improve your skills.

*See Solutions on page 143

Summary

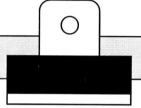

- *The 4 Stages of Learning are:*

    - *Unconscious Incompetence*
    - *Conscious Incompetence*
    - *Conscious Competence*
    - *Unconscious Competence*

- *The market place and customers' 'needs and expectations' are continuously changing. A sales process which responds to these changes is:*

    - *Motivate People to Talk to You*
    - *Help Find out Their Needs*
    - *Propose Alternatives*
    - *Ask for Commitment.*

- *It takes time and effort to go from Conscious Incompetence to Conscious Competence or Unconscious Competence.*

- *It is difficult for a salesperson at the stage of Unconscious Competence to change their behaviour.*

This is an actual job application someone submitted for a fast-food establishment (only the names have been changed...):

APPLICATION FOR EMPLOYMENT

NAME: Greg Bulmash

DESIRED POSITION: Reclining. Ha ha. But seriously, whatever is available. If I was in a position to be picky, I wouldn't be applying here in the first place.

DESIRED SALARY: $185,000 a year plus stock options and a Michael Ovitz-style severance package. If that's not possible, make an offer and we can haggle.

EDUCATION: Yes.

LAST POSITION HELD: Target for middle-management hostility.

PREVIOUS SALARY: Less than I'm worth.

MOST NOTABLE ACHIEVEMENT: My incredible collection of stolen pens and Post-it notes.

REASON FOR LEAVING: It sucked.

HOURS AVAILABLE TO WORK: Any.

PREFERRED HOURS: 1:30-3:30 p.m., Monday, Tuesday, and Thursday.

DO YOU HAVE ANY SPECIAL SKILLS?: Yes, but they're better suited to a more intimate environment.

MAY WE CONTACT YOUR CURRENT EMPLOYER?: If I had one, would I be here?

DO YOU HAVE ANY PHYSICAL CONDITIONS THAT WOULD PROHIBIT YOU FROM LIFTING UP TO 50 lbs?: Of what?

DO YOU HAVE A CAR?: I think the more appropriate question here would be 'Do you have a car that runs?'

HAVE YOU RECEIVED ANY SPECIAL AWARDS OR RECOGNITION?: I may already be a winner of the Publishers Clearing House Sweepstakes.

DO YOU SMOKE?: Only when set on fire.

WHAT WOULD YOU LIKE TO BE DOING IN FIVE YEARS?: Living in Bimini with a fabulously wealthy supermodel who thinks I'm the greatest thing since sliced bread. Actually, I'd like to be doing that now.

DO YOU CERTIFY THAT THE ABOVE IS TRUE AND COMPLETE TO THE BEST OF YOUR KNOWLEDGE?: No, but I dare you to prove otherwise!

SIGN HERE: Scorpio with Libra rising

3

Psychological Needs

As Human Beings we have certain Psychological Needs and these needs must be respected when selling to someone. If you violate these needs then you will not sell. Even when you have the most logical product, the best price, the fastest delivery, etc. Imagine you had the best product and the best price in your favour but the existing supplier is the customer's brother-in-law, would you still expect to sell? What is it that causes people not to buy the best product?

The three major **buying motivators**, in fact, are:

- *Habit* - the biggest motivator of all!

- The second biggest is *Emotion* – and the biggest emotional motivators are:

Fear   then   *Greed*

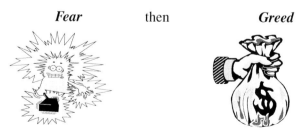

- The lowest-rated buying motivator, however, is **Logic...**

Habit

People buy from the same place time after time simply because they are in the habit of buying from that place. They are probably so relieved, the first time they find what they are looking for and not a lot of pathetic excuses! After that first successful purchase, they will put up with anything. When a buying pattern has been established people rarely alter and so repeat customers usually get the worst 'deal'. This is evidenced in many industries where we reward the behaviour we don't want. For example, think of the offers made to you if you change your mortgage to another building society. What offers are made for you to stay loyal? None. Instead, they cane you with early redemption penalties... Cancel your TV rental, do they offer you a replacement deal, maybe a reduced rate in recognition of the fact that you have paid for the set three times over already? No, a highly-trained engineer arrives in person to take back the set without a murmur! What about taking a new catalogue? You are offered £15 off your *first* order... nothing off the next ten! How about booking a holidays at the last minute? You get some great bargains, but it is noticeable how few offers there are for booking early, or booking ahead for next year, or bringing all your friends... And when did the maître d' at Burger Star show you to the best seat in the house?

In some industries, the buyer's habit is to shop around for the best deal. This usually happens when people don't buy frequently enough in one place to get addicted, or when they can't perceive any great differences – or when your store happens to be nearer. These industries are totally geared up to the prospect of losing and replacing customers. For example, a supermarket will rely heavily on your repeat buying habits. When buying a new kitchen the habit would be to shop around since we don't buy kitchens very frequently. But we all visit supermarkets at least once a week.

The supermarket companies have researched consumer behaviour. They have found that in order to change your supermarket shopping habits you only need to make 4 consecutive visits to an alternative supermarket. In order to combat this they developed a loyalty card that would record your purchases (each individual product). They can use this to identify your buying habits. A computer can be programmed to flag up when it is likely that you have paid three visits to an alternative supermarket. They could then mail you special offer coupons for products they know you buy to avoid you developing another buying habit. Makes sense doesn't it?

Imperial Tobacco calculated that it took 7 weeks to change a person's cigarette brand for life. Following trial promotions in 1989 where smokers in supermarkets were handed free packs of cigarettes, a mailing campaign was instituted to follow up a test 'cell' of triallers with free product vouchers for six more weeks. The campaign achieved 16% increase in brand switchers over the control group.

This chapter helps to develop a strategy for dealing with people who are in the habit of *not* buying from you.

Emotion

The biggest emotional motivators are Fear and Greed. The smallest is Logic.

Fear

Often customers buy for fear of losing out. They also remain with existing suppliers because of fear. If something went wrong, and they instigated the change, they would get the blame. This is the reason that Limited Period offers do work. 'Sale Must End Soon!' This is also the reason large companies use large suppliers. No one ever got fired for using the biggest and best-known supplier in the market, even if they offered the worst deal and delivered a boring, utterly predictable result. People have a fear of losing out. In buying, people buy a product emotionally and then justify it to themselves logically. Typical post-rational buyers' logic: It might have cost me more to go elsewhere. Better the Devil you know. 'Which?' magazine rated it highly. I believe in staying loyal to my suppliers. (Ha ha!) We have a policy of buying local. We have used them before and never had any trouble...

Greed

Is the corollary of fear. Fear of not having drives people to want too much. The drive to have something other people don't have. The urge to keep up with and beat the Joneses, for fear of seeming less than they are and losing face. The belief that we are what we consume... That our status in life is determined by what we have. That ultimate satisfaction can be achieved through possession of material goods. That we can 'measure' our success by piling up 'treasure'... These crazy motives are driven by fear of the alternative: failure. They are very deep down in the DNA – not at all logical. (Get rid of that old stuff at a car boot sale – see how much better you feel!)

Logic

We often think that we are being logical in making a purchase. 24 valves must be better than 16... A clockwork wind-up radio is sure to come in useful on that camping trip... I'll go by boat, the Channel Tunnel might catch fire...

In selling, however, the arguments we use to convince someone to buy our products are almost all based on *logic*. We think purely in terms of 'reasons' either to buy or not to buy. After all, why wouldn't any reasonable person buy our product? We did, we even bought the job that went with it! The secret to selling is to appeal to the emotions, but in a logical way (no one likes to feel they have bought purely because of emotion). So we need to get at the emotions behind the reasons, and to dress up our appeals to fear and greed with a logical appeal. ('Of course you'd like to be more successful at attracting gorgeous supermodels, Sir, who wouldn't?)

The psychological needs that I am going to describe in this chapter will help you to help customers to make logical decisions, bearing in mind that they may be motivated by habit or emotion.

The Minorities Rule

At this stage I need to introduce what I call the **Minorities Rule**. This rule causes businesses to run their business for a small percentage of customers rather than for the majority.

To illustrate this, I was working with an hotel which had low customer satisfaction ratings. Being part of a chain who were obsessed with customer satisfaction ratings, low ratings hurt them in every way, including in their pocket. They wanted me to help them, particularly in the restaurant area. I asked them their busiest time and was surprised to be told it was Sunday mornings between 8-9am. I decided to watch for myself what was happening.

I arrived at 8am on Sunday and couldn't believe my eyes. There was a queue of about 150 people waiting to get in to the dining room.

The queue stretched from the dining room entrance to the reception area. What were they waiting for? To eat, they first had to give their room number to the 'mobile signpost' standing at a desk. I am sure you have seen the type of desk, it usually has a sign saying 'Please wait here to be seated'. The mobile signpost was very good, he was ambidextrous and he could point to tables with his right and his left hand. But no one was eating breakfast. Not a brilliant start to the day, is it. Can you imagine what your customer satisfaction ratings would be after this experience?

When I talked to the management about this, their first reaction was to blame the customer. Most businesses do this in my experience. They said, 'We ask them to come at different times and we point out when they register that we are very busy between 8 and 9 am but they don't take any notice'.

I asked them a few more questions – all answers were approximate because, in fact, they had no idea of most of the answers:

Why did they make people wait? Answer 'To ensure no one 'steals' a breakfast they are not entitled to, we need to take a room number.'

How many guests did they have in the hotel at the weekend? – 600

Of these, how many were on a package that included breakfast? – 95 per cent!

Of the 30 people who weren't on a package deal, then, how many took a breakfast? – probably 10 -15.

Of these 10-15, if they were asked on checking out, 'Did you have breakfast this morning?' how many would lie? The managers now practised the **'Yeah/But'** technique. *Yeah/But* we can't charge them at this stage as the system doesn't allow it.' This answer seemed to put my solution into difficulty until I pointed out they already do this with the mini-bar. New answer: 'Probably 1 or 2'.

So in order to make sure 1 or 2 people can't possibly cheat them out of a breakfast they make 150 people queue! Bear in mind, the cost to the hotel of a breakfast is only the cost of the food, (staff have to be there anyway); say, less than £2. This is what I call the *Minorities Rule*. Running your business by a rigid system based on the one or two people who may be outside the loop rather than on the 99 per cent of ordinary, decent, honest, hungry human beings who make up the bulk of your customer base, and whom you would presumably like to see back again next year?

This is an extreme example and couldn't happen in your business – right? Wrong! I have yet to come across any business that does not have inconvenient systems in place because of a minority. Some are necessary; for example, banks have security glass because of bank robbers, not just so they can't hear what their customers are telling them. Certain banks won't let you pay in money at their automatic machine unless you put your card in first. This stops other bank's customers from using their pay-in facilities free. I can almost hear the *'Yeah/But'* for that one... And how about this – a bank that shall remain nameless hides the branch paying-in slips for the same reason, the rationale being that 'real' customers have paying-in slips already in their chequebooks! The fact that both these measures inconvenience their own customers to stop a few other people from abusing the system seems to be of no concern to the bank.

(In fact, banks can be truly appalling. An acquaintance records that his bank wouldn't issue a cheque card until you had been in credit with them for six months. When the day arrived and he sent off the application form (!) he was amazed to be refused a card. '£100 is a lot of money to trust someone with, and you don't appear to have a regular income', was the *'Yeah/But'*. 'I'm a self-employed contractor and I've got £9,000 in my account!' the customer protested. 'True,' said the Young Manager accusingly, 'but you could have put that money in specially, just to get a card!')

In other businesses the *Minorities Rule* is applied often because salespeople fail to sell. Let me explain. The salesperson is faced with a customer who won't buy because the company doesn't do blue widgets, only grey. The salesperson tells the sales manager, and during a performance appraisal the sales manager tells the MD. Before you know it the company has a blue widget. Doesn't apply to you? How many organisations have introduced a new product, a new range or a new variation that was eagerly awaited by the salesforce only for it to fail? Even after market research shows there is a market. You can't run a business, whatever the management consultants say, that is totally buyer-driven, most buyers just aren't worth it.

I have always run my businesses based on what I call the **'Third Principle'**. In this it is not the percentages that are important but the overall concept.

The Third Principle

One third of customers I see will automatically buy from me. This is because I have the best product, best availability, they like me, I give the best price, I'm nearest, they don't know any different, or whatever. The point is, not a lot of my income comes from *selling* to these customers. I just have to treat them nicely and they will buy from me. For this reason, I can't afford to change my business to run it just for them. There have been numerous studies to show that there is no overall correlation between Customer Satisfaction and Customer Loyalty. Very high satisfaction encourages high loyalty, very low satisfaction correlates to low loyalty. In between, however, there is no correlation. Many companies have actually increased their mid-range customer satisfaction scores and yet reduced their loyalty. So, running your business by over-investing in the top third of customers that are going to buy from you anyway (already high loyalty) is an ineffective strategy. Emotion again, rather than logic.

At the other end of the scale, one third of the customers I see will not buy from me, no matter what I do. They won't buy because they have loyalty to someone else; they don't like my product, me, my service, my location or whatever. Again, running my business in a way that tries too hard to attract these people is a disaster. You cannot sell to everyone. The number of customers who ask for a discount today is a direct reflection of the attempts of businesses to sell to everyone with price-cutting strategies that drag down the whole market, affect quality and ultimately do not produce loyal customers. This is the downside of aggressive competition in a mature market.

With the middle third of customers, however, I earn my money. They may buy from me or they may buy elsewhere. It is my ability to convert and retain these customers that I charge a premium for. I gear my business and strategy to attract these people. I ignore the bottom third, I keep the top third happy and I make money with these middle third of customers. It is the only way.

I am now going to share with you a staggering aspect of selling which I mentioned in the introduction – *Customers don't know what they want or what they need.* The reason a customer gives for not buying is rarely the real reason for not buying. This is because we buy on an emotional level and justify it to ourselves logically. Customers would feel stupid giving you the emotional reasons for not buying, so they substitute the logical ones instead. This has caused more price-slashing than any other factor. Customers often say the reason they are not buying is because of the price, when they really mean they are uncomfortable with the whole proposition only it is just too complicated to explain. The point is, there isn't a competitor in the picture at this time, only you think there is. If enough people say it, then companies think it is the price that is causing low sales, and reduce their prices. Even if, as it sometimes does, this increases the sales, you can be sure competitors are selling inferior products at what is now a higher price and making profits at your expense, because price was not the actual reason. I have seen surveys showing price was a reason for not buying but I have never seen a survey saying that price was the reason for buying!

Please don't misunderstand – price may be a reason for buying NOW! or for choosing this model over that model, or whatever. Price is just not a reason for buying, full stop.

Given the *Minorities Rule* I am sure in the following sections readers will be saying *'Yeah/But'* and 'In our business...' and will produce examples of where these things do not apply. I am sure you are absolutely right. Psychological needs never apply to everybody all the time. They apply to most people most of the time. If you understand them at a *Conscious Competence* level then you can learn to apply them at the right time.

We have a need for consistency

Our entire life is built around our need for **Consistency**. What is a table today must be a table tomorrow. What you describe as a chair I must understand as a chair. This need means we want to be consistent people. It would present social difficulties if you were my friend today, not tomorrow, then a friend again the next day.

Today   *Tomorrow*

You can see examples of *Consistency* when people gamble on the lottery. Everyone seems to bet on the lottery thinking 'this is my week'. When a £10 million jackpot is paid out to some lucky beggar you always hear people say, 'That's ridiculous, why don't they pay 10 people £1 million each?' It is only after they have bet and not won that they say that, and it's emotional reasoning, not logical, because if the jackpot is lower, fewer people put their money on and thus reduce the money available for prizes.

I have noticed as well that people don't just want to win the lottery – they want to win it exclusively! It would be inconsistent of us to bet on something we didn't think could win, and so we ignore the 14 million-to-one odds against ('*Yeah/But*, **somebody** always wins!') in order to appear consistent. It's bizarre!

How does our need for *Consistency* affect selling? Several ways:

1   Customers all think you have a poor memory (I know how ridiculous that must sound to you!)

2   They also believe that if there is nothing in writing then there is no evidence.
An amazing fact is that if you take notes people will be more truthful in their answers. That is not to say they will tell you the whole truth but if you write it down it is more likely to be closer to the truth. Try this for yourself. Make an outrageous claim about what your product or service will do. Then watch someone writing your claim down and putting your name against it as having said it; even asking you to sign it. Does that make you feel any different about saying it?

Writing notes is also a brilliant sales technique because when you are writing, you will do less talking. When you do less talking, customers do more, and when they do more, your sales will increase.

A quick question for you. Why do you write things down? You probably answered, in order to remember them. In fact we write things down so we can forget them but the very act of writing them down improves our memory. I keep a pencil and paper beside my bed. I wake up during the night and the only way I have of getting back to sleep is to write down what I am thinking about. It means I can stop thinking about it because I now know I will remember it in the morning. ('Buy extra milk'? Oh, forget it!)

3 Customers find it difficult not to buy if they have said 'yes' to the majority of your questions.

It's inconsistent to respond positively, then act negatively, so obtain as many positive responses as you can, not necessarily buying decisions. There are some questions that you can almost guarantee a 'yes' answer to. The only time they don't work is when a person is Dominant Hostile (see chapter 4 – Deal with the Behaviour) and so be very careful with them. If the customer answers 'no' to all your questions, you have made life very difficult for yourself.

- **Questions that you can almost guarantee a 'yes' answer to are:**
  A positive followed by a negative; e.g., 'Blue is a nice colour isn't it?' 'I always prefer these to those, don't you?', 'United played a blinder last night, didn't they?', etcetera.

  You can almost always guarantee a 'yes' to questions enlisting the buyer's support; e.g.,'Would you mind if I ask your opinion?' 'Can you help me?' 'Can I ask you a favour/question etc.?'

- **Questions you can almost guarantee a 'no' answer to are:**
  A negative followed by a positive, e.g.: Orange isn't very fashionable nowadays, is it?' 'Small cars aren't very convenient, are they?', etcetera. (There is a danger of obtaining 'no' answers if you appear to be agreeing with a negative previously expressed by the customer.)

4 If someone buys through habit then getting them to examine their habit will give you a chance of getting the information you need in order to break the habit.

The same principle applies to emotion. The only place you can find out this information is by asking people about their past experiences. Questions such as, where they usually buy, what is it that the supplier does for them, who is their preferred supplier?.

5 People have more desire to satisfy stated needs than unstated needs.

In Chapter 7 – Finding Out What People Really, REALLY Want, we will look at the difference between Opportunities and Needs. The reason for the difference is our need for *Consistency*. When we have stated something out loud to another person we are less likely to go back on that. Please note LESS LIKELY, that does not mean we never do, simply that we find it harder.

6 Consistency can be exploited by asking buyers whether they are looking for the cheapest price or the best product.

Not many people ever say 'the cheapest'... Cheap equates emotionally to shoddy and shows them to be unable to afford the best! After getting them to commit to this choice we are going to use another psychological need, **Conformity**, to increase the chances of them sticking to it.

7 Asking people what their role is in the organisation can exploit Consistency.

If I have a low-priced product and they tell me their role is to reduce costs, this will help me (I need to remind them of this role at strategic points).

When we look at the different buying roles within an organisation we will look at the role of the 'coach'. The way a coach works is when you say to them, 'You obviously want this product, tell me what is the best way to sell it to your manger?'. The preferred response is: 'Leave my manager to me, I can handle him/her'. Obviously you do not leave it to them. The fact that they told you that they can handle the person will increase your chances of them selling to their manager. They will try to prove to themselves that they are capable of doing so. You have a committed ally. The same tactic works with husbands and wives: 'You obviously want the product, but your partner is another story. What is the best way to sell to them?'. When a customer indicates they can control their partner then their behaviour will remain consistent with this belief. They will try to prove to you and themselves that they are 'the boss' by selling your product for you!

8 **Asking them questions about their customers in turn can identify points of Consistency.**

e.g., If a client says: 'Most of my customers are looking for prestige products to differentiate themselves socially from others', would that affect the way you handled a price negotiation/objection? Of course, the customer will be prime to buy a higher price or higher specification model and so there is more margin for the retailer. It would be inconsistent to say 'Our customers will buy more' and then try to negotiate for less.

Consistency not only applies to customers, it also applies to us. Customers look to us for *Consistency*. They look to us to be professional, on time, ring back when we say we will, look into what we promise to do, and so on. They look for *Consistency* too between our verbal and non-verbal communication; you can't make a fulfillable promise while looking at someone's feet.

They also judge your product brand value by you. If you have a top quality brand your service needs to be top quality. If not, it will affect the perception of the brand, which in turn will affect the customer's judgement of the value of your proposition.

We have a need to conform

How a society functions depends on our need to *conform*. Speak to any lawyer and they will tell you, if someone chooses not to conform to the system it does not work very well. I can't help thinking about the unfortunate person whose neighbour decided his garden was too small. The neighbour simply erected a wall 10 feet into their garden. After 10 years and numerous court battles, all of which they won, the innocent party still did not have their garden back.

They were awarded compensation but eventually gave up in despair when the compensation wasn't paid. The cost of going to court to get it paid wasn't justified. What does that say about our society and the price of non-conformity?

There was a brilliant television programme many years ago, hosted by James Burke. During the programme he stopped the action when an old lady left the auditorium to go to the toilet. Burke said he wanted to conduct an experiment with the lady as the subject. When she came back he would let her sit down before completing the section he was doing. Then he would give a signal to the audience. At the signal the audience was asked to stand up and sing 'Land of Hope and Glory' at the top of their voices.

While this action took place, a camera was focused on the lady. She was on her feet singing at the top of her voice at the same time as everybody else. Here we have someone standing and singing with no idea why they were doing it. James Burke explained that in order to remain seated whilst everyone else was standing and singing in these circumstances would take the individuality of an Einstein.

In another experiment, ten people were asked to witness a crime and then pick out the culprit from an identity parade. Nine people were taken into the confidence of the experimenters. They were asked if they would identify number 9 as the culprit even though they knew it was number 7. The question was, after nine people had identified number 9, how many people would retain sufficient individuality to identify number 7? You can perhaps imagine yourself in a line with nine other witnesses. Every other witness has identified number nine. Would you still be strong enough to remain with your view or would you begin to doubt yourself? The answer was very few people stuck to what they knew to be correct. In another famous experiment by Millgram, subjects were asked to administer successively more powerful electric 'shocks' to a 'victim' the other side of a glass screen. A white-coated 'doctor' ordered them to carry on. Most were happy to turn the dial way past the red 'lethal' mark, happy in the knowledge that they were conforming to authority, despite the despairing screams and pleas of the actor next door!

In the UK our need to queue famously shows our need to conform. I have to find a queue! If I walk into a shop or restaurant where there isn't a queue I form one mentally. I sit and say to myself, 'I was before him and after them'. Maybe you don't need to do this but I am a sad human being with a need to queue!

I worked with an organisation that painted arrows on the floor that led to their promotion product and they tell me most people followed the arrows.

In any showroom, the vast majority of customers will turn left as soon as they enter the store and they will tend to go round clockwise. I find non-conformist shoppers who contra-rotate in stores quite irritating! Many furniture showrooms shepherd people around with huge, brightly-coloured signs. Entrance doors and exit doors are a way of witnessing *Conformity*. People rarely exit through entrances and vice versa. Supermarkets are designed to maintain a more-or-less constant rate of circulation that passes by as many products as possible.

In business, the need to conform is very useful. Have you ever had to ask a question that people sometimes respond to, by questioning why you need to ask it? e.g., home telephone number, car registration, etc. 'Standard business practice' will save many explanations. (It's often to do with insurance, or fire regs., but more usually it's our old friend, data capture...) Why, for instance, does my local DIY store always ask my post code, even when I pay with cash? I dread a mailshot, but it hasn't come yet.

Another way to use the need to conform is to get customers to close themselves! If you are going to a sales meeting, try pre-preparing a meeting agenda.

The last item is always: 'Agree Future Action', or: 'Agree Time Scales'. Instead. how about putting in: 'Agree Delivery Schedule'? At the start of the meeting you hand a copy of the agenda to the client. If you say, 'I have been thinking about our meeting (that in itself will differentiate you from other salespeople!) and I have prepared an agenda. Is there anything you would like to add?', clients will very rarely remove items from your agenda and when they get to the last item, I assure you, they will close themselves!

I used the principle of *Conformity* with an organisation that normally took sales orders with multiple lines. The average order contained 5 different items and so we had order forms printed with a red line after the seventh line on the order form. The salespeople were instructed what to say if any customer asked what the red line was for (they usually did when signing the order form). They were to tell them that the line indicated their target and also the average number of items usually ordered. You would be amazed at how many customers tried to reach the red line. The average number of lines per order increased significantly.

When using the need to conform, keep non-verbal communication completely consistent with verbal communication. For example, if everyone in the world bought from us at full retail prices, if all our communication was consistent with that then few people would ever ask for a discount! This is why nobody ever asks for a discount in Tesco's. Very few people want to be different. (It always amazes me how, when you are selling a valuable service, the customer immediately tries to cut your price; yet he would not dream of arguing with his greengrocer over the price of a bunch of bananas, or tell the plumber how much to charge for fixing a leaking pipe.)

Paying a deposit is another area where people conform. Salespeople who get problems with deposits are almost always asking for it in such a way as to give a clue they don't always get one. Ask for a deposit as if everybody in the world paid in full. More people will pay the deposit and will pay a larger percentage than they do now.

Salespeople sometimes use the need to conform by implying the customer cannot afford the item (asking the customer to conform to the role of shopping for what they can afford). It isn't a very pleasant experience for the customer. People will often complain about the way they were treated by a salesperson who uses this tactic. Although they complain, however, they often still buy the product! (Please note: I would not advocate this use of *Conformity* and use this example merely to explain the power of the concept. As we learn from the Bible and the story of Cain the wild hunter killing his brother Able the settled farmer, we are mostly either one or the other. I believe the art of selling is to achieve an overall balance between hunting and farming, and so too much aggressiveness in exploiting people's desire to conform in the long run damages goodwill and does not help me achieve my long-term goals.

There is a connection between the needs for *Consistency* and *Conformity*. If customers commit themselves to something they will want to be consistent with that commitment. If they don't or won't make a commitment, then they may conform to what most people do, that is, walk!

The attractiveness of scarcity

Everyone wants what everyone else wants, and nobody wants what nobody wants. Think of Christmas. It's either Cabbage Patch Dolls, Tellytubbies, Furbies, or whatever. Every Christmas, something is in short supply. It's a situation deliberately created by the manufacturers. They restrict the supply and that stimulates even further demand. So does this only affect children? Not a bit of it! I don't know why it creates a demand but I first became aware of it in about 1976 when there was a 'sugar shortage'. If you are too young to remember it, I cannot be sure if there really was a shortage but I do remember people rushing out to buy sugar. Demand was stimulated so much that supermarkets restricted purchases to two bags per customer. This in turn created a stampede! The whole family had to go shopping, each to collect their two bags.

What implications does this have for selling? One problem for some companies is their Unique Selling Points (USPs) work against the attractiveness of **Scarcity**. They advertise huge stocks, 24-hour opening, instant 0% credit... Training courses on Customer Care have even advised organisations to structure themselves in a way that nothing ever appears to be in short supply, they think it is bad for the business image.

In order to trigger a 'buy now' decision, the salesperson however needs to create an image of *Scarcity*. Contrast: 'Yes you can order at any time, we have 6 left' with: 'I am afraid I will have to have a decision as we are down to our last 6'. When a client asks me for a meeting I always refuse the first date because I am working with someone else. If it is really important to them to have the meeting on that date I can usually rearrange my prior engagement for them. In this way I can judge the importance of the meeting to them and by being scarce I am more attractive to them. (I used to do this but since many clients will read this book I don't do it anymore!)

There is always a seasonal reason for doing things now. Christmas and everyone's busy, Spring and people are on skiing holidays, Easter and schools have broken up, etc. There are sales, optimum times, busy times. Even normally quiet times when you will get the best deal and so everyone wants to do business now. The point is, if there is no reason for ordering it today, why order it today? Most salespeople think these 'reasons' sound a bit unbelievable (and usually they are false). What they need to do is think in advance of some real reasons for doing business now! I find ours to be a society increasingly bent on instant gratification. When people want something, they will buy it *now*. When was the last time you went into Sainsbury's and said: 'That looks like a tasty new breakfast cereal, I think I will try that out next time I come shopping'?

Scarcity is a powerful concept and you need to be entirely consistent with being busy. That means every contact with a customer should reflect that you are busy.

You will arrange more meetings at quarter to the hour than on the hour. Something psychologically tells us a meeting arranged for 11 o'clock will take us up to lunchtime.

Quarter to the hour psychologically leads people to believe the meeting will take a shorter time. An experiment showed the impact of words when people witnessed an accident. If they were asked, 'What speed was the red car doing when it crashed into the blue car?' they would give a higher speed than if asked 'What speed was the red car doing when it made contact with the blue car?'. Red is a more aggressive colour than blue, so red cars must be driven faster! 'Crashed into' is a more emotive phrase than 'made contact with'. The principle for meetings at a quarter to the hour is exactly the same. It sounds less threatening; and, being before the hour, at the same time more positive.

If a customer says they 'need to think about it', how about trying: 'Sure it's a big decision. Can I show you this one which is almost as nice, in case the one you really want is gone before you come back?'

People have a need to reciprocate

In short if you do something nice for me I will do something nice for you. If you make it harder for me I will make it harder for you. **Reciprocation** is why 'No Obligation' offers still make most people feel obligated. (Charities often give people the option of putting a stamp on the post-paid reply envelope. It works every time!)

An example of when salespeople make it harder for customers is with not giving out information. For example plans, quotations, etc. Salespeople who retain plans or put only a little information on a quotation to make it harder for customers to shop around are just not thinking straight (*Unconscious Incompetence*).

Imagine you were considering buying something that has a substantial cost, say £2,000. Would you ever buy it without considering other options and suppliers? What if the salesperson made it difficult for you by retaining plans? What if they made a quotation so vague that you couldn't explain to the other shop exactly what you were quoted for? Would this make you say to yourself: 'Woe is me, I will have to go and buy from that nasty man who has made it difficult for me'? Does anyone do this? If not, why do salespeople continually play this type of 'trick'? Probably because of the Minority Rule! Some customers will abuse the gift of information and use it to find a reason not to buy – not all, but some. They use you for ideas and buy elsewhere more cheaply. I heard a camera shop complaining about this: 'Customers come in here, ask for our advice and then go and buy in Dixon's!'.

The fact is, you can never sell to everyone. If you changed your system to be more helpful to customers who shop around you will find more people coming back to you. Most salespeople have heard, 'I'd like to buy from you but I have a lower quotation'. In this case, at least you have a chance of getting the business; if you make things difficult, people will reciprocate and not give you a second chance. I use the need to reciprocate to increase the chances of people coming back (see Chapter 9 – Addressing Concerns).

Have you ever been in a shoe shop and the assistant has about twenty boxes of shoes out looking for the right pair for you? You wonder why they bother having a stockroom! If you are like me, the only reason they are still opening boxes after closing time is because I am desperate to find something I can buy... I can't leave without buying a pair, so they've got a guaranteed sale, if only they could find the right product! The need to reciprocate doesn't make everyone buy – just most people. It can sometimes also work against you because, if you don't buy, it can be harder to go back into that shoe shop next time because of the feeling of obligation towards that poor assistant.

The important thing is you will never stop people shopping around. Trying to make it difficult for people simply means you are not using the need to reciprocate to your advantage. You are also applying the *Minorities Rule*, making it harder for everybody because a few people might abuse the information you freely give them.

The examples above may appear to apply to retail but this applies in all selling. I worked with an insurance broker who would try to restrict information given to clients for the same reason. Quotations are the same, whatever industry you are in.

There is of course another aspect to this business with quotations. Imagine again that you bought something costing £2000. When you get home to wait for delivery of your 'treasure' what do you do? Of course, you get out the paperwork. The invoice reads: 'To supplying and fitting one xyz'. Does that look like £2000 to you? For £2000, in order to remain consistent, I would want a long list so that it looked like £2000 worth. Invoices and quotations should be as detailed as possible.

Doesn't that make it very easy for someone else to give a quote on a like-for-like basis? It doesn't, 'actually'. What it does, is it helps the competitor give a 'similar' or 'equivalent' quote. You will find even with commodity items there are very few competitors who stock exactly the same as you. When the competitor salesperson starts talking about 'similar' and 'equivalent' items it begins to sow the seeds of doubt. The customer should know, because you should tell them, that you could also supply cheaper (correct use of the word Cheap – see Chapter 8 – Propose Solutions) by substituting 'equivalents'. Most customers are not trying to buy cheaper 'equivalents', or 'me-too' products as they are known, they are trying to buy exactly the same but for a lower price.

If you combine the attractiveness of *Scarcity* with the need to reciprocate then you have a very powerful selling tool.

If *Scarcity* is used on its own, though, people mistrust you. It's a bit like Del Boy saying, 'Only one vase left, luv', when he has just bought a job lot. Using: 'I will do something for you and I don't do this for everybody' is much more successful. Difficult to do, but whoever said 'You need sincerity and when you can fake it you have it made' was probably right. I would advocate being sincere and not conning. It is always possible to find a way of doing something in a special way for someone, and the fact that you are going to profit from their gratitude should not get in the way of you being genuinely helpful. One good turn deserves another.

The most important way that *Reciprocation* affects us is that if we want customers to trust us we need to start by trusting them. Think of car dealers, do you trust them? Do you feel trusted by them? If you had forgotten your chequebook when collecting your car after a service, what do you think they would do?

An example of how I have used the need to reciprocate came in the Motor Trade. I was working with a car dealer who had problems in his Service Department with rubber cheques that would frequently bounce. (This was a franchised dealer who normally dealt with cars less than 4 years old. You would think the owners were able to afford servicing!). Because of cheques bouncing they added-in to the system that if customers didn't have a cheque card then the service manager would have to authorise the cheque. Unfortunately the service manager was no better at intercepting cheques that would bounce and they still had the problem. I advised them to carry on as before with only one change. After the receptionist got authorisation they should go back and say, 'I couldn't find the sales manager but I am sure you won't let me down so I will take a chance on you. Please don't get me the sack!' Because the receptionist was making it easier for the customer the customer would reciprocate and the cheques stopped bouncing completely.

I told this story to a non-franchised dealer one day; he told me that he could count on one hand the number of times a cheque had bounced in the 15 years he had been in business. When I looked at his processes it was clear he trusted his customers and that is why he wasn't let down. He doesn't apply the *Minorities Rule*. He does have some cheques that bounce because he said, 'count on one hand', but he doesn't let unusual events inconvenience the majority of customers. I can hear people saying 'But you can't trust people in our neck of the woods' and I am sure you are right. If you can't trust people then you are not to be trusted, right? As long as we all play by the same rules...

The biggest obstacle to using *Reciprocation* is Sales Managers. They often seem to make rules that prevent salespeople from using the customer's need to reciprocate to their advantage. I don't know why this is. Sales Managers seem to focus on why they don't get sales and almost ignore why they do get sales. Think of a salesperson who provides information for a customer that seems to make it easier for them to shop around. If they do not get the business then the Sales Manager will see the cause as the information the salesperson has 'given away for nothing'. They will often put in a system to prevent the salesperson from giving out plans, putting full information on quotes, etc.

It is sometimes difficult to see how not making it difficult for customers to shop around will make it less likely that they will. I assure you that in the vast majority of selling situations this is true. Don't apply the *Minorities Rule* because a few customers might abuse the information. You probably had no chance of getting their business in the first place. An example of this need to reciprocate is again with supermarkets, large signs saying 'We check the prices so you don't have to'. 'Find the same product cheaper elsewhere and we will refund twice the difference'. This makes it easier to buy now with confidence and it also shows huge confidence in your own products and prices. A story in the paper told about one family that spent its time going round all the local supermarkets comparing prices. They were making a nice living from 'twice the difference' refunds, until the manager of one local supermarket cleverly cut his losses and put them on the payroll!)

Enthusiasm is infectious

The only thing more infectious than *Enthusiasm* is un-enthusiasm. The difficulty for British people is we are not naturally good at singing the praises of anything. All our social conventions are based around things being 'not bad', rather than 'Grrreat!'. At best, things are just 'OK'. This upsets English-speaking foreigners, Australians, Americans and the like, no end. Naturally enthusiastic people, they just can't understand that when we say, 'Sure, Jim, it's not looking too bad at all', we aren't damning their efforts with faint praise, or demonstrating our innate superiority, but underneath that British 'sang froid' and behind the 'stiff upper lip' are really 'over the moon' with delight!

I collect oxymorons (an Oxymoron is two words which are often said together but don't really go together, such as 'pretty ugly', 'airline food', 'military intelligence', etc.) and you will find hundreds of them in our language used in order to avoid sounding over-the-top in our *Enthusiasm* for anything good. In selling, however, customers expect you to be a bit OTT (another figure of speech with a long Greek name is Hyperbole, or over-exaggeration, and this has given us the word 'hype') and are genuinely infected with gloom and disappointment if you are not. In my experience, people interpret everything you say as one level down, so:

Absolutely Brilliant	is heard as...
Brilliant	is heard as...
Good	is heard as...
Satisfactory	is heard as...
Poor	is heard as...
Unbelievably Bad.	

It works in reverse, with customers having a complaint. Salespeople hear:

Unbelievably Bad	is heard as...
Poor	is heard as...
Average	is heard as...
Better than average	is heard as...
Brilliant	is heard as...
Bloody marvellous...	

Good system huh? The trouble is that if you don't understand the system then you can't play the game. I have met salespeople who wanted to be completely honest. I believe in being honest, but they wanted to be suicidal. It has never worked. I am in favour of using at least one level up all the time; in my experience it is the only way.

We have a need to visualise

In order to purchase a product or service we have a **Need to Visualise** ourselves owning it. Hence the success of what is lovingly referred to as the 'Puppy Dog Technique'. What happens here is the owner of the puppy dog lets you take it home to see what the family thinks. The owner knows when the family sees it in their house there is little chance of you taking the puppy back. This works because of the *Need to Visualise* and also the need to reciprocate, they are making it easy for you to make a decision. My wife buys antiques from a certain dealer; he remembers her name, which is worrying. If there is anything that Julie indicates she likes, they deliver it to see how she likes it when it's in situ... It doesn't always work but it does improve their chances of a sale. By the way, because they show trust, they leave it without deposits etc., and they make it easy for her, she reciprocates by not negotiating hard enough - despite my training!

The success of helping people to *Visualise* is evidenced by the increase in Computer Aided Design (CAD) facilities and Internet links in many showrooms, for instance kitchens. The trouble is, most salespeople only use such aids when the customer has already almost bought the product. The *Minorities Rule* applies...

'*Yeah/But* you can't do it for everybody can you?' (I mean you couldn't make an appointment for most people at a quiet time and use it to invoke the need to reciprocate, could you?). 'Everybody would abuse it and most of them are just using us for ideas they can take down to the DIY store...'.

If you don't have CAD, what you can do is ask some questions which help people to *Visualise*. An example of this would be, in a showroom, when someone is looking at a bed, if you ask them: 'If the bed was in your bedroom, where would the door be?'. Any question about how they would integrate the ownership of the product or service within their existing lifestyle will help people to *Visualise* themselves owning the product.

If you are selling a service, it is much harder still for the buyer to *Visualise*. In some cases it could be that all they would see is a series of meetings, which is enough to turn off even the most hardened business customer, even a Marketing Manager... You must paint a picture of the outcome, not the process. It is absolutely no good showing even an engineering model or artist's impression, and saying, oh well, this isn't actually what you will be getting, it is a bit like this only better/bigger/brighter/more sort of bluey-coloured... People can only buy what they see, not what you see. And most of the time, they will only see what they want to see.

We have a need for praise

We all actively seek approval for what we are doing. No matter how often we try to tell ourselves it doesn't matter. The fact that we often have to tell ourselves uncovers how much it does matter. In selling, it is important to support people and to be sincere. You can always say, 'It is not my taste but I can understand how much you like it'. In my experience salespeople don't need me to teach them about **praising** people, they only need to be taught to do it sincerely. They also need help to stop them from criticising.

When faced with a quiet person we often finish their sentences and we often interrupt. When they make a decision, we tell them the decision is wrong. When they tell us what they know, we often tell them they are wrong.

For example in the bathroom industry, I watched a salesperson deal with a 'Submissive Hostile' type of customer who said, 'I want a traditional close-coupled WC with a pipe between the cistern and the....' Not only did the salesperson interrupt at that point, they also finished the sentence and told the person they were an idiot (they used more subtle language but the effect was the same) because as anyone knows, a close-coupled cistern doesn't have a pipe...

Why, oh why didn't they say something like: 'You have obviously been looking around, you know what you want and that makes my job a lot easier.' This uses *Praise* and *Conformity* because they will now try to conform to the behaviour of a person who knows what they want. It doesn't matter if you call it close-coupled or a bunny rabbit! If that is what the customer wants, just point to it and they will be happy.

How about, when someone makes a decision, trying: 'You are obviously very decisive.' You will be amazed at how often they will try to conform to that label. In my experience the hardest problem to deal with in selling is indecisiveness. Give me someone who makes decisions any day, even if they are the wrong ones. I have other techniques for dealing with wrong decisions, but for the moment I want to praise their decisiveness.

When someone says I want '*x*'-type, and you know '*x*'-type is incompatible with their need, you can say: 'You have obviously researched into this, which helps me a lot, but someone has given you the wrong information'. Blame someone else for giving them the wrong information, not them for giving it to you.

When a customer makes a comment I like to tell them they are obviously shrewd businessmen/women. They will take this as praise and then want to conform to this image. My entire presentation is geared around the fact that any shrewd businessperson would be mad to pass up this opportunity.

Whilst working on a course I had just completed a session on the need for praise when we went to the dining room for lunch. Spaghetti Bolognese on the menu and I asked for a spoon. The waitress responded 'The Italians use a knife and fork you know!' and the way she said it demonstrated perfectly how she wanted to criticise. I suppose as salespeople we have a need to impress the customer with our intelligence and knowledge, but if you look carefully you will see many examples of people using it the wrong way to merely seem superior.

Think of the following:

2	**+**	**2**	**=**	**4**
7	**+**	**2**	**=**	**9**
6	**+**	**2**	**=**	**8**
3	**+**	**3**	**=**	**6**
2	**+**	**5**	**=**	**8**
1	**+**	**5**	**=**	**6**

If you are the same as millions of other people the chances are you said to yourself, '2 + 5 = 7, not 8'. Very few people ever say to me, 'well done, you got 5 right'! People only focus on the one I got wrong.

Salespeople can't afford this luxury. Finding something to praise is a lot harder than finding something to criticise and that is why it is all the more powerful, because people don't often use or receive praise.

We have a need to take turns in conversation

We learn turn-taking from a very early age. There is evidence of infants as early as three months old having learned to **take turns**. By this I mean that in normal conversations we prefer them to be structured by you saying something and then I say something. We prefer this structure to one where one person talks without giving the opportunity to reply. You can observe this procedure in virtually any conversation. If you watch carefully, you will be able to observe the signals we send when we think it is our turn to speak.

Some of the signals are:

- We make an audible inhalation sound that gives the other person a clue we are going to say something.
- We may lean forward.
- We may point with our finger or hold up our hand in order to enter the conversation.

Try observing some of the signals in action. We also send signals when we think it is the other persons turn to speak.The most important one to watch for, that I have come across, is that

- We stop talking! Then,
- We may raise our eyebrows.
- We may nod our head.
- We may lean forward.

This turn-taking has important implications for us particularly in addressing Concerns. If we stop talking, customers will start! If a customer wants to take their turn and gives us the signals and we don't let them the effect is the same as if we had interrupted them. We saw in Section 4, there are some people we shouldn't interrupt!

Summary

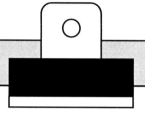

- *The 3 Most Powerful Buying Motivators are:*

  - *Habit*
  - *Emotion*
  - *Logic*

  ...in this order.

- *The two most powerful Emotions are:*

  - *Fear*
  - *Greed*

- *The only way to break Habit is to use the Psychological Needs:*

  - *Need for Consistency*
  - *Need to Conform*
  - *The Attractiveness of Scarcity*
  - *Need to Reciprocate*
  - *The Infectiousness of Enthusiasm*
  - *The Need to Visualise*
  - *The Need for Praise*
  - *Need to Take Turns in a Conversation*

Prison Problem...

Three men in prison are given a fighting chance by the guard. He lines them up as follows facing a wall. He tells them they are wearing between them 2 white hats and 2 black hats.

The rules are:

• They must face the wall so they are not allowed to turn round and look at anyone else's hat.

• They must not look up at their own hat.

• There are no breaks in the wall nor can they see over it or round it.

• They are not allowed to talk to each other.

If any one of them can give a logical reason whereby they know the colour of their own hat, they can all go free. They are not allowed to guess.

How did they go free? *(answer on page 143)*

4

Deal with the Behaviour

If I ask you to think of the worst salesperson and showroom in your area, then imagine a customer walking through the door. What names might this salesperson use to describe that individual? I have run this exercise many times on training courses and believe me I have heard everything, for example:

- A Time Waster (this is the most common)
- A DIY'er
- An Arnie (who says, 'I'll be back' and doesn't)
- 'Be-backs' (as above)
- A Know-all
- A Skinflint
- A 'Something for Nothing'
- A Nerd (especially if wearing sandals)
- Brochure Hunters
- Chatterboxes

However it is expressed, this concept of a 'time waster' never ceases to amaze me. Someone gets out of bed, dresses, jumps in their car, pays for a parking space and enters a showroom, *only to waste the salesperson's time?* The people who use the expression 'time waster' should do a spell of cold calling. They would realise that anyone who takes the trouble to enter your premises, even if only to get out of the rain, is a warm prospect.

Unless you expect to sell to *everyone*, it is impossible to waste your time. It has been estimated it is at least 5 times more expensive to get a new customer than to keep an existing one. Since the most effective form of advertising is word of mouth then the least you can do is some advertising. It's funny but people who use 'time waster' all seem to have converted a small sale into a bigger one. It may have been a car to someone who only came in for a windscreen wiper or a bathroom suite to someone who came in for a washer. They never seem to connect that maybe, just maybe their behaviour causes some customers *not* to buy from them.

A business owner wandered into a Jaguar showroom. Creative type, he wore jeans. The posh-suited salesman looked him up and down, mostly down. 'I am looking for a new company car but I have a budget of only fifteen thousand, can you help me?' The salesman muttered something about there being a couple of part-exchanges round the back. 'Yes, I saw those, but I prefer the newer, slightly more rounded-looking version' said the customer, looking around vaguely. 'That model hasn't changed in fifteen years', snapped the salesman. 'Oh, well I have obviously made a mistake' said the customer, and wandered out again. Next day, he bought a Mazda.

If you ask customers to list the words that would describe the way they want to be treated by salespeople then the list usually includes things such as:

- Important
- Knowledgeable
- A serious buyer
- Friendly
- Streetwise (not gullible)
- Able to afford what they want.

Everyone I have run this exercise with agreed they could keep in their head the negative 'labels' we sometimes give customers and still deal with the customer appropriately – although not one of them claimed to be an expert in body language. We instinctively feel that we can keep one view of customers in our head whilst dealing with them in a totally different way. I think this is unlikely if not impossible. Have you ever been a buyer and felt that the salesperson was treating you as if you were a time waster? What makes people think they are better than others at hiding what they really think? Our body gives messages we are unable to conceal (unless of course you are at *Conscious Competence* for non-verbal communication).

Because we filter information through labels the filter ensures that our label was correct. For example, let's say a 'friend' says they like your hair, you will probably be quite pleased. If someone whom you consider 'dislikes' you says it, however, then you may well feel that they are not being truthful.

In fact I demonstrate this to groups. I give secret instructions independently to two groups at opposite sides of a room, to one group that I am a 'friend' of a delegate and to the second that I 'dislike' the delegate. I then tell the delegate that I like their jacket, tie, etc. Now, both groups have witnessed the same body language. They heard the words said in the same way and they heard the exact same words– yet they still have two opposing views of the situation. The first group mostly sees the interaction as me passing a compliment, the second group as me being patronising. If we apply this principle back to the labels we sometimes give customers, then does your behaviour change because of the labels you give them?

Most people are now saying to themselves, 'I can understand the adverse effects of doing that. I'm going to stop labelling people'. Well I have some news for you! I would advise you *not* to stop labelling people. In fact it would be very dangerous for you to stop labelling people. If you are walking down the street and someone comes towards you brandishing a gun, label them as angry or mad very quickly. If they turn out to be going to a fancy dress party, labelling them as a terrorist won't be too serious a mistake. We label people all the time because of their dress, manner, voice, what they are saying. It saves us a lot of time and mostly our labels are right. In most situations the consequences of getting it wrong are not serious.

In my experience, however, most people tend to label on the negative side. Given the existence of mad gunmen, this is a relatively safe position (which may be why, on the above exercise, I get more negative than positive labels). But we need to be more circumspect when we label people, as in the true story above, a person wearing jeans and knowing nothing about your products is not necessarily wasting your valuable time!

The consequence of wrong labelling in selling can be very

detrimental to your success. I was training a salesman in Australia who told me confidently he could tell immediately someone came in the showroom whether or not they were going to buy today. Whoopee Doo! The challenge in selling is to sell to these people, not to make certain they won't buy, by treating them immediately they walk in the door as if they won't.

How can you use this positively? If you increase the number of positive labels you use, for example:

- Nice
- Interesting character
- Knowledgeable
- Astute
- Streetwise
- Affluent

...you will be amazed at how many nice, interesting, knowledgeable, streetwise, astute, wealthy people you will meet!

Another aspect of labelling behaviour is our tendency to judge ourselves by our *intentions* and others by the *results* they achieve. If at work you do something wrong the chances are you will analyse your behaviour in terms of your intentions. 'I got it wrong but I was trying to do the right thing'. We don't give others that benefit because we can't see their intentions, we can only see the results they achieve. Think of a company you know that is poorly managed. Does the staff in that company give the management the benefit of their intentions? They will complain about the results the management team achieve. I don't know of a single manager, who turns up at work in the morning and says to themselves, 'I wonder how I can stuff up this company today?'. In my experience, 99 per cent of company managers and employees turn up at work wanting to do a good job and to be recognised for doing it.

The power of labels

It is important to understand the power and problems of labelling because I am now going to label customer behaviour and I would like the behaviours to be seen in a positive light to help people deal well with customers.

The most fundamental skill in selling is the ability to treat each customer as an individual. In my coaching sessions I sometimes wonder if people are reading from a script. They are using a script of course. It may not be a formal, written-down script, but they have used it before and they do practise it. In fact they seem to practise it with everybody. Wouldn't it be useful to consider which types of customers are likely to be loyal, which are 'price sensitive'? Which customers want you to give them information (facts and figures) and which would like your opinion? I have also seen on many occasions a salesperson struggling to 'warm the customer up' because someone told them it was the right thing to do. I have also seen some customers cringing, not only at the attempt to warm them up but because they don't welcome non-business-related conversations. I think 'warm up' is likely to have the opposite effect on these people.

'Assertive behaviour' appears to be a current buzzword and there seems to me to be some confusion over what assertive behaviour is. If you look up the word Assertive in a dictionary you will find definitions such as: dogmatic, insisting on one's rights and opinions, thrusting one's view forward or being forthright. These definitions are as far away from what I would consider to be assertive behaviour as is possible. I need to give some indication of my definition of Assertiveness. It is easiest to do this by distinguishing from Aggressive and Submissive behaviour.

Aggressive behaviour

This is where a person only considers their own rights and has no consideration of the other person's rights. If you look at the dictionary definitions above you will find these are all about considering only your rights. This is why I consider these definitions to be those of Aggression, rather than Assertion. Incidentally, if you look in a dictionary at what 'aggressive' means, the word 'assertive' also appears. One technique I have read for being assertive is the broken record technique (constantly repeating your point of view as if the record was broken). If you try this for yourself I think you will find out it is an aggressive technique simply by the response you get when using it.

Submissive behaviour is where a person only considers the rights of others. Again in dictionaries you will find definitions such as: giving way, yielding, obedience etc.

Assertive behaviour is where a person considers not only their own rights (Aggressive) but also the rights of others (Submissive). You can respect that other people have rights while retaining your own. The model I am going to consider is a practical way of achieving assertive behaviour. Some people will need to be listened to in order that you respect and understand their point of view. Some people will need help from you to identify and articulate their point of view.

So let us consider a **behavioural model**. This model is loosely based on the work of the Swiss psychologist, Carl Gustav Jung (1875-1961). Reasons for considering it to be a *behavioural model*, rather than a personality model, are:

- If it were easy to identify the personality of customers then the companies that sell Personality Questionnaires would quickly go out of business.
- Most psychologists would agree that it is very difficult or impossible to change someone else's personality. As a selling tool it would, therefore, be useless. I know from my own experience that you can change someone's behaviour while leaving their personality intact!

In fact, behaviour changes throughout the selling cycle. How you start dealing with someone is not necessarily how you would want to finish. Behaviour can change rapidly. An example of external factors causing rapid behavioural change is on the motorway. Imagine you approach a bridge and on the bridge there is a stripey-looking car with a light flashing on top – Police! Everyone who is speeding (and even some who are not) is observed to rapidly change their behaviour, even when it is only the Motorway Maintenance vehicle after all.

You may remember from Chapter 1, how most communication takes place at an unconscious level. I would like you to consider how you communicate with people displaying different behaviours.

Bringing this to *Conscious Competence* level will enable you to deal with more people more effectively. In addition, if anything changes then you will know how to deal with it.

The first behavioural aspect I would like to look at is Dominance. Write in the box all the words that imply Dominant Behaviour to you.

Dominant

Note that by doing this exercise for yourself you are defining dominant in your own terms. If I asked my subordinates whether I am dominant they may respond 'Yes – Very!' and if I asked my boss she might say 'No'. What they are defining is their relationship to me. This means that when you deal with people you don't follow someone else's rules you deal with them in relation to yourself.

Next, consider Submissive Behaviour. Write in the box all the words that imply Submissive Behaviour to you.

Submissive

It may help to consider whether some behaviour stems from the need to achieve results quickly. If a person wants a specific result quickly then they may behave in a dominant fashion. If however they want any result they can get, they may behave in a submissive fashion. The need to get specific results quickly will be a determining factor in how we deal with them.

Next consider Warm behaviour. Write in the box all the words that imply Warm Behaviour to you.

Warm

Warm behaviour stems from our need or involvement and trust of others.

And finally, hostile behaviour.

Hostile

To give an indication of how to deal with these two behaviours we have conflicting needs for Independence and Involvement. Warm behaviour comes from the need to be involved and perhaps you have recorded words, which show that need. Hostile behaviour is a result of our need for independence and stems from mistrust.

We now have a *behavioural model*:

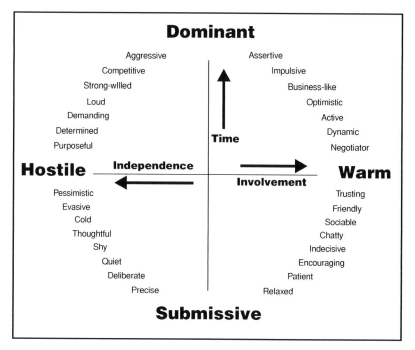

This may reflect some of the words you have used for the four behaviours. We can look at the four sectors and categorise the behaviour and therefore the strategy for dealing with the behaviour.

The four behavioural categories are:

1. Dominant Hostile
2. Submissive Hostile
3. Submissive Warm
4. Dominant Warm

I have worked my way anti-clockwise and I suggest that as you do the following exercise you work in the same way. I will explain the reason for this at the end.

The four types of behaviour are usually quite easy to recognise:

1 Dominant Hostile

Examples of situations where someone is likely to behave in a Dominant Hostile manner:

- A complaint.
- Buying a product in an industry where they have had a bad experience.
- Buying a product in an industry that they consider to be dishonest.
- When they are being forced to use your services; e.g., your subsidiary company that must use you rather than having a free hand.

How to spot the behaviour:
- There will be mistrust and the person may make that mistrust obvious (e.g., by saying, 'don't give me any of your sales patter').
- They will be impatient.
- A lot of telling you the answers in advance and pressuring you to answer quickly.
- Cynicism about your product, service, prices or everything.

2 Submissive Hostile

Examples of situations where someone is likely to behave in a Submissive Hostile manner:

- As for a Dominant Hostile; i.e., a complaint, bad previous experience, etc. (although they will not tell you of their mistrust).
- Very early in the buying cycle, when they want to research products and avoid being sold. (They may agree with everything you tell them at this stage in order to get out without entering a discussion.) In Performance Appraisals staff often behave this way and it takes a good manager to open them up.

How to spot the behaviour:
- There will be mistrust and the person will not make that mistrust

obvious unless you carefully watch their body language.

- They will try to avoid you.
- There will be lots of silences and they may appear to be listening too intently.
- They will not challenge or question you about the product or service but thank you effusively at the end.
- They may surreptitiously do things that indicate lack of trust; e.g., they may mark the spark plugs and oil filter of their car when they put it in for a service, seek confirmation of your movements from third parties or query receipts.

3 Submissive Warm

Examples of situations where someone is likely to behave in a Submissive Warm manner:

- When they have lots of time on their hands or they are lonely.
- When they are undecided.
- Very early in the buying cycle when they want to research products and trust the industry. They want to ask salespeople for their advice.
- At the hairdresser! They can't put it back on, can they?

How to spot the behaviour:
- They may combine not objecting with not buying.
- They may talk a lot but not say anything.
- There will be a lot of detailed questions about the product and what you think.
- They will be complimentary about your product and agree all its good points will be extremely useful. Their *Enthusiasm* about the product can appear to be higher than the salesperson's.

4 Dominant Warm

Examples of situations where someone is likely to behave in a Dominant Warm manner:
- A long-term loyal customer you know well.

- Buying a product in an industry where they have lots of trust.
- When they are looking for support from you; e.g., a dodgy complaint.

How to spot the behaviour:
- They tend to use your first name.
- They will enjoy banter and like to barter about the price. They like to negotiate.
- They will be open about what they think they need.
- They may challenge for evidence of the ability of a product to perform because they would like to believe it is true.

If you don't deal with them appropriately, then all people can easily change their behaviour. For example the Dominant Warm who thinks they know what they want. If you don't listen to them carefully they may quickly become Dominant Hostile!

A director agreed to let a rep from a multi-level marketing operation present to the board of his small business. The MD welcomed the rep politely enough,but reminded him he had fifteen minutes to make his case. The rep launched into a lengthy dissertation on the 'profit motive'. After ten minutes, the MD rather icily asked him to get to the point: what was he selling? Unflustered, the rep ploughed on. After fifteen minutes, the increasingly impatient MD interrupted him again: 'We don't need to know about profits, we run a business and we're losing money right now. We just want to hear what you are selling.' The rep carried on as if nothing had happened. At that point the directors all got up and walked out, leaving the poor guy pattering on to himself.

The worst scenario for a salesperson is for a prospect to behave in a Submissive Hostile way because if they leave and don't buy, and don't even tell you why, then you have lost. So, if you lose, don't lose the lesson!

Now the question is how are we to deal with them? I have six questions for you to consider:

1   What questioning style would you adopt for this type of person?

Many studies have been made on whether 'Open' or 'Closed'

questions are more successful. Some have shown that they are and some have concluded the opposite. My own research shows that overall the most successful salespeople use a balance between open and closed with slightly more closed (55 per cent closed to 45 per cent open). This is overall and when you look at it in terms of this model it is clear that with some customers they focus on open and with some they focus on closed questions. No type of question should be used exclusively.

A Closed question is one that gets a specific piece of information; e.g., 'what is the capital of Italy' or, 'do you prefer front or rear-wheel drive cars?' An Open question is one that is designed to continue a dialogue; e.g, 'what do you think about '*x*'?'; 'how would you feel if '*y*'?'; 'can you tell me about '*z*'?'. Note that people don't always (or even often) answer a closed question with a closed answer. If you ask, 'Do you have any hobbies?' people rarely answer with either yes or no. They would normally say something like 'Yes I play golf, snooker, read books', etc. The main difference in response to open or closed questions is when someone wants to hide information from you.

After a closed question it is much easier to hide information.

A study of interviewing techniques, by Geiselman et al. (1985), showed that people are more likely to make errors with information when asked closed questions. This may help when deciding what type of questions you would prefer to focus on. You should consider:

- Whether you should focus on open or closed questions and would this change at any time?
- Whether your question would be straightforward and the customer would readily know the answer.

Otherwise you may wish to ask a question that the customer would really need to think about. Both types need to be relevant.

Everyone will get frustrated when a salesperson asks stupid questions. If the reason for the question isn't obvious then you should give the reason for asking it along with the question; e.g., 'We need to consider whether the use of your house will change in the near future, do you have any teenage children?'(There is a connection somewhere!)

2   Would you interrupt this person?
Or perhaps, should you interrupt this person! You should consider:

- What if they are off-track or just plain wrong?

3   What would be the likely effect of a short gap in the conversation?
You should consider:

- Would this be a good thing or should you prevent it by avoiding short gaps?

It is interesting that a spectogram study by Vivien C. Tatler (Language Processes 1986, p 210) showed that in fact there is very little silence in normal conversation. If there is a short gap someone will fill it! The real question is, should you fill the gap or should you leave a short 'pregnant pause' for them to fill?

4   Should you give this person your opinion?
You should consider:

- What would you do if they asked for it?

5   What about 'small talk' or 'warm up'? Would they want it and should you try?

6   How loyal and price sensitive are these people?
For this question you will need to consider habits of behaviour or personality. This is because we have looked at behaviour as situationally driven and when people buy their behaviour will obviously change. People who buy are normally behaving either Dominant Warm, or Submissive Warm. The question is should you treat someone continuing to behave in this way as loyal or price sensitive?

Complete the following boxes with how you think you should deal with people who are behaving this way. There are no right or wrong answers and the main benefit of doing this exercise is that if you do come across people who behave this way then it makes sense to think about how to deal with them in advance.

Dominant Hostile

1. Questioning Style:

2. Interrupting

3. Short Gap in the Conversation

4. Your Opinion

5. Small Talk

6. Loyalty and Price Sensitivity

Submissive Hostile

1. Questioning Style:

2. Interrupting

3. Short Gap in the Conversation

4. Your Opinion

5. Small Talk

6. Loyalty and Price Sensitivity

Submissive Warm

1. Questioning Style:

2. Interrupting

3. Short Gap in the Conversation

4. Your Opinion

5. Small Talk

6. Loyalty and Price Sensitivity

Dominant Warm

1. Questioning Style:

2. Interrupting

3. Short Gap in the Conversation

4. Your Opinion

5. Small Talk

6. Loyalty and Price Sensitivity

I have carefully observed the effects of different strategies for dealing with the above behaviour. The following guidelines have not only worked for me, they have worked for people I have trained. When analysing things that haven't gone well in a selling situation we have almost always traced the start of problems to not following the 'guidelines' within this model.

Problems fall into one of two categories:

- Dealing with someone based on their personality rather than their behaviour; e.g., a Submissive Warm as a Submissive Warm whilst they were behaving in a Dominant Hostile manner.
- Recognising the correct behavioural type but adopting the wrong strategy.

You should also note that the strategy for dealing with people might change depending on the situation. People have often said to me that if someone is behaving in a Dominant Hostile fashion they interrupt them and tell them to calm down or they will refuse to deal with them. This may be OK in a complaint situation, but certainly will not work if you don't already have their money! They will walk out or hang up on you.

Dominant Hostile

Remember, the drivers of this behaviour are: the need to get specific results quickly, and the need for independence.

1. Questioning style

Focus on Open questions at the beginning. This recognises their need for independence and gives you the opportunity to make them feel you value their contribution. It is difficult to ask Closed questions and avoid making assumptions. They will also appreciate questions they haven't thought of, that they should consider. Frame all early questions in the future tense; e.g., 'What will happen if market demand changes?' 'How do you see the account operating?' They are at least likely to have thought of the consequences or potential pitfalls of future actions. They get annoyed with questions about the past!

2 Interrupting

Never interrupt a Dominant Hostile. they will feel you are challenging their authority and not valuing their input.You will provoke comments like: 'If you will only just listen I was getting to that.' Worse still they may move to Submissive Hostile and leave without buying or telling you why.

3 Short gap in the conversation

The most likely thing is that you will jump in to fill the gap and you must avoid that, however anxious you may be to respond or gain control of a worsening situation. Taking a breath, pausing for effect, emphasising a point, just getting to the main point, lost their train of thought, remembered the milk... doesn't matter, speak too soon and you are interrupting! Your only chance is to let the gaps run on. Nod wisely! Mirror their emotions with your expressions. Maintain eye contact. Don't worry about silences, when it is 'your turn' to speak the Dominant Hostile will soon remind you...'Well, what do you say about that, then?'

4 Your Opinion

When a Dominant Hostile wants your opinion they will ask for it (and even then they don't really want it!). When your partner asks if you like their dress or their new suit, they don't want to hear your opinion, they want you to confirm theirs! You may want to divert the question; e.g., 'Well, I have my view of course but it is more important to focus on what you want'. Another technique is to refer to previous experience: 'We tried that before and what happened then was...' get on to facts, the Dominant Hostile wants to hear facts, not opinions. Try to avoid using the word 'think', they don't want to hear: 'I think we can deliver 5,000 by Friday', they want you to go and find out. Get as quickly as possible to planning a course of action. Think in bullet points.

5 Small talk

These people don't need to be warmed up, they are already at boiling point! Stick to business, be professional, have the facts at your fingertips, don't be cowed, maintain eye contact and you may find that after a while, they suddenly melt and start saying embarrassingly nice things instead ('I can see you're a man after my own heart!') It's hard to keep a furnace going without fuel.

6 Loyalty and price sensitivity

Treat Dominant Hostiles as being non-loyal and price sensitive. They will only continue to do business with you if they have good logical reasons. Don't worry, they understand the common laws of business, probably better than most. Handling price objections is usually straightforward provided you are logical and factual. They may hand this process over to a subordinate. Woe betide the salesperson who uses illogical arguments based on poor knowledge with a Dominant Hostile. These people can be human shredding machines you will never forget meeting. (Robert Maxwell was a classic case who even terrified his own children.)

Submissive Hostile

The driver for this type of behaviour is not being under pressure to get results quickly. They don't like to make a mistake and they want their independence to be recognised.

1 Questioning style

Focus on Open questions at the start, for the same reasons as with the Dominant Hostile. Submissive Hostile behaviour is keeping information from you and Closed questions make this easier. You need answers to have something to work with. They will bounce back any tricky questions; e.g., Q. 'What would you like to happen now?' A.'You're the expert, you tell me...' For this reason, frame early questions in the past tense, so they already know the answers and feel OK about telling you. 'What have you done with orders like this before?' 'How well did that work for you?', etc. These questions help them explore their needs in safety. You could try a leading question: 'Which is better for you, '*x*' or '*y*'?

2 Interrupting

Never interrupt a Submissive Hostile as they are at their most dangerous when their independence is threatened. They will stop giving information or worse, leave without buying or saying why. Submissive Hostiles like to leave gaps in the conversation, these are elephant traps where even your body language can make them feel you are impatient to interrupt, confirming your view of their lack of status. A Dominant Hostile will tell you to stop talking, but a Submissive Hostile will merely *wish* you would...Give them plenty of thinking space, avoid direct eye contact, and watch for that sudden switch to Dominance - when they walk out on you!

3 Opinions

The Submissive Hostile is unlikely to ask, since they don't trust you, but just in case they do, you haven't got any, OK!

4 Small talk

Is a good idea in moderation. You need to try with this one. Make it non-threatening and non-standard; i.e., don't burble on about the weather or how you got stuck in traffic on the B4975. Try to read up on the market and react to what is happening in the news. 'Will the situation in Colombia affect your business?' 'I see that Sterling is falling against the D-mark, that must be good for your exports', etcetera. They will be flattered that you have such a high opinion of their views.

5 Loyalty and Price Sensitivity

Perhaps surprisingly, Submissive Hostiles are very loyal and not at all price sensitive. They do shop around a lot, because they need to be in control (submissive behaviour means not trusting salespeople and remember, they hate to make a mistake.) They have time to do research themselves (they don't trust anyone else) and so are often called Brochure Hunters. When they do find someone they can trust, however, they stop shopping. They don't really enjoy shopping, and neither do they enjoy being approached by salespeople, who they feel are there to undermine their decision-making capability. They will be acutely aware of every sales technique in your locker, and eager to trip you up: try being an un-sales person for a change!

Submissive Warm

This type of behaviour is driven by the need for involvement. They are uncertain about the product or service and display lots of trust. They also have time to research. Do they have the buying decision, though?

1 Questioning style

This person will answer most questions in an Open fashion. You need to use Closed, leading questions to get them to stay on the subject. The funniest thing in selling is when a Submissive Warm salesperson meets a Submissive Warm customer... four hours later they are driven by the need to get something done before closing time and so at last get on the subject!

It is really important to change your questioning style at the end otherwise they can combine not objecting with not buying. To close this person you need Open questions, e.g., 'How would you feel about moving on to the next stage?' The 'sales funnel' where you ask Open questions to open subjects and Closed questions to close them is completely reversed.

If this person feels you won't like an answer or they may say something stupid, they may **bounce** the question: 'Q 'Which would you prefer?' A. 'I do't know. I need to think about it.' For this reason, it is important to stay in the past. 'How long have you been looking for '*x*'?' 'What did you like about your previous '*y*'?' Compliment them on their answers; you are not going to make them feel stupid.

2 Interrupting

This person will probably not notice you interrupting if you do it nicely and not too often. A degree of firmness is appreciated and you will need to interrupt if you plan to sell to them. Conversations between friends are full of gentle interruptions, it is a natural part of Submissive Warm behaviour to volunteer thoughts and to be open with information, sometimes of a personal nature! Practise nodding sympathetically! Two words of caution, though:

- Don't interrupt while they are on the subject! The more relevant information people give you the more chance you have of selling to them.

- You may get a Dominant Hostile husband and a Submissive Warm wife together, or vice-versa. Don't interrupt or the other partner will take sides and you'll be 'pig in the middle'. If you wait long enough, they are sure to do all the interrupting for you ('Shut up and listen to the man, he doesn't want to hear all that!') The partner will usually keep the talker on the point.

3 Short gaps in the conversation

There won't be any. Submissive Warms feel threatened by silence. Get them to open up with gaps in your own presentation.

4 Your opinion

They welcome your opinion, but be sparing. They need reassurance: 'What would you do in my place?' ' What's the best thing to do now?' Back up your opinions with plenty of evidence, however. You're the expert! Use positive language, never admit to not being certain or to there being several options. If in doubt, tell them: 'I'll need some more information from you before I answer that one. Now, have you ever...?'

5 Small talk

Absolutely – this is the reason they buy and you should not waste it. My rule is, the sandwich principle: small talk at the beginning and at the end, but stick to the facts in the middle.

6 Loyalty and price sensitivity

Submissive Warms stay loyal to whomever they are talking to at the time. *Close them or lose them...* Though they will eventually stray, they are prime for selling long-term loyalty packages and product enhancements.

Dominant Warm

This behaviour comes from the need to get things done quickly and the need for involvement.

1 Questioning Style

Try to balance your questions. Too many Open questions and they will see you as an interrogator, a threat. Too many Closed, and you are making assumptions, not recognising their need for involvement. Challenging, relevant questioning is a demonstration of your professionalism. Stick to the future tense ('*Will* you be doing '*x*'?', 'How do you see this shaping up?'). Minimise questions on points of fact, Dominant Warms hate time wasters and can become Hostile with people who haven't done their homework.

2 Interrupting

OK, provided you don't do it too often. They would expect you to interrupt rather than let them waste their time by going off at a tangent.

3 Short gaps in the conversation

Are most likely to be friendly pauses for reassurance. Don't rush in, on the other hand don't let them go on too long, remember, they're letting you be in charge – up to a point!

4 Your opinion

Dominant Warms are after facts, not opinions, although they may ask out of politeness. Be ready to back up anything you say with facts, particularly clever ones! After all, you're the expert...

5 Small talk

Again, not too much. It's okay to start the meeting by breaking the ice, but be ready to get down to business. Watch for their body language and know when it's time to move on.

6 Loyalty and price sensitivity

Dominant warms are loyal (so long as you stay on the right side of them) but they are price sensitive (and sharp with it) so you need good explanations for differences in prices (e.g.: 'But last time you said it would cost '*x*'...?' 'Can we just run through these figures again...'. They will expect good product knowledge to justify price differences and won't appreciate you reading out loud from the company product brochure.

Overall, the easiest 'character' to work out, and work with. Will give you a sympathetic hearing but doesn't suffer fools gladly. As far as your techniques are concerned, a 'little bit of everything' is OK, which is why I have put this one last, just to cheer you up.

Deal with the behaviour

This model of the four different behavioural types is, in my opinion, the most important in selling. I hope you can see the importance of dealing with the behaviour, not the person. Understand, too, that most people are not always one type or another, but may cross over between types during the course of a meeting. The Submissive Warm type of person can sometimes be reminded of what a 'pushover' most people consider them to be, and of how they felt 'ripped-off' in the past. Expressions like: 'I have had my fingers burned before' are a sure sign that they are gearing themselves up for a burst of Dominant Hostility, although they are not very good at it! Let them get on with it, don't interrupt. Don't try small talk or any of the other 'rules' for Submissive Warms – it could be dangerous. But it will soon blow over!

I would advise you to brush up on dealing with Submissive Hostile behaviour. It is the most profitable and has the biggest impact. This is because salespeople find it the hardest behaviour to deal with and are the least capable of dealing with it. Your competition is relatively light! In addition they are the most loyal and the least price sensitive and so when they trust you, they will be a customer for life.

In summary, the following charts will help you deal assertively with all different behaviour types.

Behavioural type:	Dominant Hostile	Submissive Hostile	Submissive Warm	Dominant Warm
They want:	Respect information	Independence	Advice	Results Banter and Barter
You should talk about:	Relevant details Facts Evidence	Past experiences Benefits	What everybody does Features	Benefits Features
You should avoid:	Unsupported claims	Pressure Future questions	Impatience	Irrelevance Waffle Complexity
Remember:	Listen Use silence Don't interrupt	Praise them Don't finish their sentences	Connect on a personal level	Expect negotiation Keep the sale moving

Words to Use

Dominant Hostile	Submissive Hostile	Submissive Warm	Dominant Warm
Explain	OK	Together	Results
Proven	Advantageous	Enjoy	Achieve
Maintain	Independent	Advice	Immediate
Evidence	Useful	Gift	Benefits
System	Expertise	Help	Manage
Step by Step	Long Term	Experience	Control
Reason	Experienced	Special	Rewards
Value	Trusted	Warm	Innovative
Effective	Tested	Lovely	Fast Acting
Compared To	Straightforward	Happy	Easy
Features	Reduce	Sensuous	Convenient
Increase	Save	Everybody	Gain
Maximise	Proven	Satisfaction	Improve

Summary

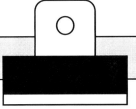

- *Yes, label people, it saves time – but...*

- *Use positive rather than negative labels.*

   We judge others by the results they achieve but we judge ourselves more by our intentions. (The best example of this I suppose is a football match. As supporters, we make brilliant strikers...) This leads us to be unnecessarily negative about people who need our help and support.

- *The Four Behavioural Types are:*

   - *Dominant Hostile*

      Concentrate on asking Future Questions only and give facts rather than opinions.

   - *Submissive Hostile*

      Concentrate on Easy Open Questions about the past and cope with the periods of silence.

   - *Submissive Warm*

      Ask easy leading questions and offer your opinion.

   - *Dominant Warm*

      Don't give your opinion until asked. Ask questions about the future

The New Priest

A new priest at his first mass was so nervous he could hardly speak. After mass he asked the monsignor how he had done. The monsignor replied, 'When I am worried about getting nervous on the pulpit, I put a glass of vodka next to the water glass. If I start to get nervous, I take a sip.'

So the next Sunday he took the monsignor's advice. At the beginning of the sermon, he got nervous and took a drink. Thus fortified, he proceeded to talk up a storm. Upon return to his office after mass, he found the following note pinned to his door:

- Sip the vodka, don't gulp.
- There are 10 commandments, not 12.
- There are 12 disciples, not 10.
- Jesus was consecrated, not constipated.
- Jacob wagered his donkey, he did not 'bet his ass'.
- We do not refer to Jesus Christ as 'the late J.C.'
- The Father, Son, and Holy Ghost are not referred to as Daddy, Junior and the Spook.
- David slew Goliath, he did not 'kick the shit' out of him.
- When David was hit by a rock and knocked off his donkey, please don't say he was 'stoned off his ass'.
- We do not refer to the cross as the Big T!
- When Jesus broke the bread at the Last Supper he said, 'Take this and eat it, for it is my body', he did not say, 'Eat me.'
- The Virgin Mary is not referred to as Mary with the Cherry.
- The recommended grace before a meal is not: 'Rub-A-dub-dub, thanks for the grub, yeah God!'
- Next Sunday there will be a taffy-pulling contest at St. Peter's, not a peter-pulling contest at St. Taffy's.

5

Decision Makers

According to a Financial Times survey 'HOW BRITISH BUSINESS BUYS', there is a real need for salespeople to make more effort to speak with decision influencers. Their survey found the following:

Size of company (Number of employees)	Average number of decision influencers	Average number of decision influencers *who talk to salespeople*
less than 200	3.43	1.72
201-400	4.85	1.75
401-1,000	5.81	1.90
1,000 +	6.50	1.65

As you can see, the larger the company, the more powerful (hence, unapproachable) is the Buyer. But all is not lost, it may merely mean that the Buying function is more dispersed within the organisation. When you do meet a Customer, you have a once only, never-to-be repeated opportunity to find out the buying system. Ask at the first opportunity: 'Tell me, this is the first time I have dealt with your company, what is your purchasing system?'

Good salespeople have a system for recording such information as name, job title, telephone extension., best contact times and days, lunch hours and other personal information; e.g., birthday, family birthdays and hobbies.

Keep trying to find within the company, the following types of buyers:-

The Economic Buyer

...signs the cheques and can veto any purchase. There is only one economic buyer and for this reason it is critical to find out who gives the final 'yes' for your sale.

The User Buyer

...uses the product themselves. Their focus is therefore much narrower than the economic buyer's. The User Buyer will ask you about areas of immediate, day-to-day concerns, such as product reliability and service record.

The Technical Buyer

Their role is to screen out. They make recommendations, they cannot say 'yes' but they can say 'no'. Give them time and respect.

The Coach

...can be found in the Customer's organisation, in your own organisation, or indeed outside both. They provide and interpret information about the situation, influence buying decisions and adjudicate how each person can win. Your tactic for dealing with this person is to join them - 'how can we pull this off together?'.

When I first learned to sell, you had to find THE MAN... That is, the person with the MONEY, the AUTHORITY – and the NEED. This is no longer appropriate. In these days of empowerment, dispersed budgets and flatter management structures, etc., there are more decision influencers than previously. I liken the need to find out decision-makers to a golf tournament – you cannot win a golf tournament at any individual hole but you can lose it at every hole.

Treat everyone in an organisation as a decision influencer. It can take months to get a new customer but it takes only seconds to lose one. If they are not the decision maker, treat them as a coach and use the strategy of getting them to help you to sell to their company. If you are respectful and helpful to people they will reciprocate and help you to sell to their company.

Summary

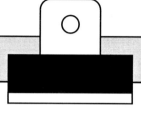

There is a need for salespeople to speak to more decision influencers. The four Decision Influencers are:

- *The Economic Buyer*

- *The User Buyer*

- *The Technical Buyer*

- *The Coach*

More Church Humour...

Actual Announcements from Church Bulletins

1. Don't let worry kill you – the church can help.

2. Thursday night - Potluck supper. Prayer and medication to follow.

3. Remember in prayer the many who are sick of our church and community.

4. For those of you who have children and don't know it, we have a nursery downstairs.

5. The rosebud on the altar this morning is to announce the birth of David Alan Belzer, the sin of Rev. and Mrs. Julius Belzer.

6. This afternoon there will be a meeting in the South and North ends of the church. Children will be baptised at both ends.

7. Tuesday at 4:00 p.m. there will be an ice cream social. All ladies giving milk will please come early.

8. Wednesday, the Ladies' Liturgy Society will meet. Mrs. Jones will sing, 'Put me in My Little Bed' accompanied by the pastor.

9. Thursday at 5:00 p.m. there will be a meeting of the Little Mothers Club. All wishing to become Little Mothers, please see the minister in his study.

10. This being Easter Sunday, we will ask Mrs. Lewis to come forward and lay an egg on the altar.

11. The service will close with 'Little Drops of Water.' One of the ladies will start quietly and the rest of the congregation will join in.

12. Next Sunday a special collection will be taken to defray the cost of the new carpet. All those wishing to do something on the new carpet will come forward and do so.

13. The ladies of the church have cast off clothing of every kind and they may be seen in the church basement Friday.

14. A bean supper will be held on Tuesday evening in the church hall. Music will follow.

15. At the evening service tonight, the sermon topic will be 'What is Hell?' Come early and listen to our choir practice.

16. PENSIONERS WED - Fifty years of friendship ends at altar.

6

Motivating People to Talk to You

All selling depends on this stage. Without the ability to motivate people to talk to you it is impossible to sell. Imagine: General Custer is fighting Chief Sitting Bull at his famous Last Stand. A salesperson approaches...

Salesperson	'General, nice to see you – how's business?'
General	'Who in the Sam Hill are you?'
Salesperson	'Can you spare me a few minutes?'
General	'Are you selling something?'
Salesperson	'Well I would like to take up a little of your time to show you something new.'
General	'I'm sorry, I am rather busy right now.'
Salesperson	'If I could just explain? It will only take a few moments.'
General	'Can't you see I have a war to fight? I haven't got time to talk to you.'
Salesperson	'Well I think I may have something that would be of use to you'
General	'I have already told you. I have a war to fight, I haven't got time to talk to you.'
Salesperson (turning away despondently)	'OK, sorry to trouble you. But I do have this new thing called a sub-machine gun, I am sure it could help you!'
General	'Say, son, would you mind removing this arrow from my...'

Without the ability to motivate people to talk to you I think you would need to have the equivalent of a sub-machine gun. You would also need to demonstrate it quickly!

So how do you motivate people to talk to you? I have been told many times that you need to 'warm up' a prospect before getting down to business. In my experience the guidelines for dealing with different behaviours still apply. For example I think the way to 'warm up' a Dominant Hostile is to get down to business quickly and stop faffing about!

There are some techniques that will help. Avoid saying:-

- 'How's business?'
- 'What a lovely goldfish tank you have in reception'
- 'Isn't the weather lovely?'
- 'Can I help you?' – unless of course you are dealing with another customer at the time and you want this one to say, 'No thanks, I'm just looking'.

Good things to say are:

- *Surprising*
- *Intriguing*
- *Funny*

For example, in a showroom, if you walk up to a customer and say, 'Do you know, it's amazing...' - nobody (unless they are very deaf) will ever reply, 'No thanks, I'm just looking'! In business, if you say, 'Do you know, a funny thing happened on the way here?' it is very difficult for someone to show you the door. You could also ask a guaranteed YES question (see Chapter 4) 'Can I ask your opinion/ advice/help?'

The best salespeople seem to respond to what is happening. Cold calling on the telephone, I have said to people: 'I am sorry, you have caught me completely off-guard!' (Pause for the intrigue.) 'I was expecting a voice mail!'. If this is said with the right tone with a smile you can get into a nice, light conversation straight away.

I think the beginning of any business meeting should give a logical business reason for speaking to you and a reason for them to answer your questions. I also like the advice to start with:-

You
We
I

I find it really difficult to work this order of priority into an actual presentation! I think it is another of those ideas that sounds logical but is difficult to do in practice. I cannot imagine myself saying at the end of our meeting that *you* should be more knowledgeable about *our* products! The concept, however, of making the meeting for the benefit of the customer first, both of you second and me last, is a good one. I can and do say, 'I have been thinking about our meeting and have prepared this agenda. Is there anything *you* would like to add?'

Other ways of motivating people to talk to you are things everybody is aware of but few people do:

Smile

It is particularly important to smile before saying something nice rather than after. Try doing it both ways and see the results you get. My observation is that people seem to get a message saying it is insincere if you verbalise an emotion and then show it.

Use Positive Language

Saying 'Great' instead of 'Not bad' and 'Excellent' instead of 'OK', etc. makes you sound more enthusiastic (see Chapter 3 – Enthusiasm is Infectious)

Adopt an air of success

...without being overconfident, being busy and not wanting to waste their, or your own, time; nevertheless, first impressions count and success rubs off, so why not rub off a successful first impression!.

Try using humour
(I use humour a lot but this won't work for everyone...)

Body Language

A lot is written about body language and I am sure it is useful. (You can probably see me shuffling my chair and crossing my legs as I write this...) In every book I have read about the subject, however, there is something different and even contradictory. In body-language 'speak', touching your nose is said to mean you are not comfortable with what you are saying. I have noticed it can also mean a fly has just settled on it! Crossing your arms is supposed to be a sign of defensiveness, but what else are you supposed to do with them when you haven't been invited to sit down or given a drink? It should reassure the other person that you are not about to hit them... I am not in favour of reading too much into body language.

If you are getting negative signals, the danger is that you will filter everything through a negative label, as we discussed in Chapter 4. A technique I do use is mirroring the person's body language. I think this does develop rapport and is easy to do. This technique involves you adopting the body language position of the person you are talking to and following (subtly!) their movements. You may then equally subtly start to make more open, friendly or submissive gestures and they will unconsciously follow you. (Don't imagine that waggling your finger in the air will persuade them to sign the order, however!)

Most people do agree that maintaining eye contact is important and some people find this difficult to do, so here are some tips.

First, though, I believe that overly direct eye contact is actually threatening. You only have to look at children staring each other out, or boxers at a weigh-in, to see how uncomfortable direct eye contact can make people. People who fix you right in the eyes while they are droning on at you and never once blink or look away appear mad. A study by McGurk and Macdonald (1976) showed that in fact, rather than maintain eye contact, most people are watching your lips, not your eyes. They need to concentrate on your lip movements, to hear better what you are saying. Otherwise, there is a slight lag in perception, like you get when a film soundtrack is out of sync. with the picture.

If you find it difficult maintaining non-threatening eye contact, then my tip is to try to concentrate on the person's mouth rather than their eyes. This is less threatening to both people. At normal conversation distance it is almost impossible to tell whether someone is actually looking at your eyes or your mouth. You can then shift your gaze slightly to meet their eyeline directly when you want to emphasise a point, or when you are smiling at them, and it comes across as genuine and sincere communication!

The only body language signals I really look out for are:

Anything pointing up! I have found that this is a good signal, and it has never let me down. I believe that when people point up it is a very good sign. For example, when people steeple their fingers like this:

Or, even, are pointing up like this:

Some books say these are not positive signs and may be signs of indecisiveness. It may be a self-fulfilling prophecy but when I see them I think people have decided to buy. This principle hasn't let me down (so far!).

In any event I think looking at body language and deciding that signals indicate negative messages about what the person is thinking, is very dangerous.

Body space, or rather lack of it, is a way of destroying rapport quickly and I have found salespeople to be remarkably insensitive about body space, especially when dealing with people less tall than themselves. It can be quite fun to watch someone being pushed around backwards, I am sure you have seen it at parties. A person needs a body space of say 2'6" to feel comfortable and they are talking to someone who needs only 2'. The person who needs 2'6" moves away slowly only to be closed up by the person who needs only 2'. The only person who doesn't seem to notice is the person who is too close! The effect is one person moving slowly backwards and both people on a tour of the room. The opposite is also true; moving away from someone who wants to get closer is not a good rapport developing technique.

Body space works like this:

We can get quite close at the sides to a person, as most body space is needed at the front. The space needed at the rear is less but this is not particularly important in selling. If you are invading their body space or vice-versa, try moving to the side. Show a brochure or something. You will probably find you can even make physical contact with people without threatening them, if you approach from the side.

Talking about physical contact, there is a high correlation between touching customers and selling to them. This is why shaking hands is so important. It is also possible to touch people in other ways without them even being aware they are being touched. I demonstrate this on courses by touching everyone on a course during day one and telling them I have done it on day two. I do this by touching them in a non-threatening way, perhaps touching their arm as well as shaking hands, perhaps touching their elbow when I am directing them somewhere. Tapping their arm before I ask them a question... I think there is a useful, non-threatening area between the shoulder and the fingertips.

You can touch this area without people being consciously aware that you are doing so. The small of the back is also OK, when you want to steer someone, say into a lift; but this is an unconscious 'control' gesture that could offend someone of higher 'status' in an organisation.

A word of caution, be very careful with touch between the sexes. In my part of the country if a female touches a male anywhere other than on the upper arm it can be seen as a 'come on' signal. Kissing is definitely out on a first meeting!

However, when dealing with prospects from other countries the protocols can be different. Best to take advice, otherwise you could misinterpret that sloppy bear-hug or the whiskery peck on three cheeks as a sign that Ilya or Maçiek fancies you rotten! This is another reason to mistrust 'body language' as a science, it varies so much from country to country (watch an Italian driving!).

The best way of motivating someone to talk to you is talking about something that interests them. I would recommend reading the Dale Carnegie classic, *How to Win Friends and Influence People*.

Asking general questions about their company, what they make, where they sit in the market place, how it is structured, etc., is non-threatening, particularly for a Submissive Hostile or Submissive Warm. A Dominant Hostile or Dominant Warm may expect you to have conducted some research on this before your meeting. It is a good idea to go on to the Internet and print out all the background information from their site in case this approach is rejected. Dominant people will respond better to questions about where they want to go and the challenges that are facing them over the next 5 years. The fact that you actually want to know, and appear to believe that they know the answers to these questions, is highly flattering to their ego!

Now you have motivated the customer to talk to you and to answer your questions the next stage is to decide what questions to ask.

Summary

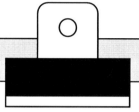

- *Avoid saying:*

  - *'How's business?'*
  - *'What a lovely goldfish tank you have in reception'*
  - *'Isn't the weather lovely?'*
  - *'Can I help you?' (unless of course you are dealing with another customer at the time and you want this one to say 'No thanks, I'm just looking').*

- *Good things to say are:*

  - *Surprising*
  - *Intriguing*
  - *Funny*

- *Smile*

- *Be Positive*

- *Have an air of success.*

- *Use humour if you can.*

- *Watch for anything pointing up (well, almost anything...).*

- *Be Careful with Body Space.*

- *Use non-threatening touch in order to develop rapport.*

Dilbert Quotes

A magazine recently ran a 'Dilbert Quotes' contest. They were looking for people to submit quotes from their real-life, Dilbert-type managers. Here are some of the submissions (with no apologies):

- As of tomorrow, employees will only be able to access the building using individual security cards. Pictures will be taken next Wednesday and employees will receive their cards in two weeks.' (Winning entry from Fred Dales at Microsoft Corp. in Redmond, WA.)

- What I need is a list of specific unknown problems we will encounter. (Lykes Lines Shipping)

- How long is this Beta guy going to keep testing our stuff? (Programming intern, Microsoft IIS Development team)

- E-mail is not to be used to pass on information or data. It should be used only for company business. (Accounting Mgr., Electric Boat Company)

- This project is so important, we can't let things that are more important interfere with it. (Advertising/Mktg. Mgr., UPS)

- Doing it right is no excuse for not meeting the schedule. (R&D Supervisor, Minnesota Mining & Manufacturing /3M Corp.)

- My boss spent the entire weekend retyping a 25-page proposal that only needed corrections. She claims the disk I gave her was damaged and she couldn't edit it. The disk I gave her was write-protected. (CIO of Dell Computers)

- Quote from the boss: 'Teamwork is a lot of people doing what I say.' (Mktg. executive, Citrix Corporation)

7

Finding Out What People Really, REALLY Want!

The stages of need

I have seen many different explanations of the buying process and my favourite is the simplest. Before making a buying decision customers will go through the following stages:

Unaware of the Need

They may be unaware that they have a need for the product or service itself. Or, they may be unaware of the need to buy it from you, at that price, at that time, etc.

Aware of the Need

Self-explanatory.

Analyse the Impact of the Need

Is it worthwhile buying the product or service? This is the stage where most sales are lost. If the customer considers this stage without any assistance from the salesperson then there is no selling taking place, only facilitating people buying, which is not the same thing.

Decide Response to the Need

Are you going to buy or do without?

Decide the Buying Criteria

What type of widget will you buy and what colour, etc?

Choose the Supplier

Having recognised the need and fixed the criteria, who will you buy from?

The stages can actually be taken in any order but when the process is experienced in a random order people feel vulnerable. In this case they have a tendency to mistrust any advice. Customers will trust salespeople who take them through the buying process in this order.

At what stage is the *price* of the product relevant? Customers ask about price and try to negotiate at all stages. It is critical to selling and price negotiation to know what stage the customer is at. For example if you are unaware of the need does it matter what the price is? Browsers will often ask for the best price and sellers panic and offer discounts at this stage. This destroys the attractiveness of *Scarcity* and damages trust at the same time. A request for the best price is only an invitation to sell *Scarcity*, quality and other virtues.

When customers analyse the impact of the need, the price is relevant. The price now has to exceed the need... A good salesperson will ask questions that help the customer to evaluate the price of the need.

Logically, the need has a constant value – although the customer's perception of the need changes.

The buying decision will be based totally on the perception of the value of the need.

Let us look at the typical sales pitch. Listen carefully to the questions asked by a salesperson and most of them will be questions that help them to sell to you. This creates mistrust since I do not want someone to sell to me; I want help to make the best buying decision.

What are the types of questions that would help you sell to someone in your business? Let me give you some examples of different industries:

A bathroom showroom will ask:

- What style do you want?
- What colour do you want?

Given the answers to these questions and enough money you could find yourself with a bathroom suite. The same applies with:

A car dealer:

- What model do you want?
- What colour, package, etc.?
- When do you want it?

An airline:
- Where do you want to go?
- When do you want to travel?
- What class of accommodation do you want?

It is because this is the information that you need in order to sell to someone that this type of question creates mistrust. What goes on in my head when I am asked these questions is that the salesperson wants to sell me their best fit with my answers. It may be that using this approach I will get the right product for my needs, but only if I know the answers to these questions – like passing an exam! In most selling situations the customer does not know the answer. In a buying situation, of course, the customer would know the answers to these questions. If you know where you want to go, you buy a ticket. If you know what car you want, you buy the car. Selling takes place, as opposed to negotiation, when the customer needs help to find out what they want.

At this stage I would like to draw the distinction between knowing what you want and thinking you know what you want. There are many occasions when a customer would speak to an order taker who would ask questions similar to the ones above. The customer would end up with what they asked for only to perhaps find it is the wrong product.

For this reason I call the above type of question the **Salesperson's Agenda**. This is because these questions elicit only the information that the Salesperson needs in order to sell to you.

To identify a *Salesperson's Agenda* question, ask yourself: 'What is the minimum information I would need to let you buy something from me'? It may not be the right product for you, but if you asked me and gave me only that information I could take your order. If you currently start with, or introduce early in the selling process, these types of questions then you are destroying trust with the customer. This is because you are trying to sell the customer something rather than helping them to buy.

The *Salesperson's Agenda* is the reason why the original subtitle of this book was 'Buying Without Tears'. If you are buying and you follow my system for finding out your needs, by using the **Customer's Agenda**, then you will find out your real needs. You may change your mind about who to buy from, but you will make fewer mistakes.

If a *Salesperson's Agenda* question destroys trust, what type of question will build trust? To answer this we need to look at the *Customer's Agenda*. What sort of things would a customer want to know before deciding that they will buy from you? For me, everything centres on *trust*. They trust you:

- Not to sell them something they don't want or need
- To listen to them properly
- To do what you say you will do
- To charge a reasonable price
- To respect them even after you have their money
- That the product or service will perform as promised

Let's take a careful look at these points of trust. It may seem that some of them are obvious or that some are difficult, if not impossible, to achieve. How, for example, can you get a customer to trust that you will respect them after you have their money? I believe all the secrets to selling are contained here. *If you can do these things why would anyone not buy from you?* Remember the minorities' rule – not everyone will buy from you but at least most will.

This is how to sell to emotional people. All you have to learn is how to stop someone buying something that they don't really need or want. To do this you need to ask the right questions and listen to the answers.

Sounds easy? Then consider this:

Questioning of the correct type is not easy. I have recorded thousands of questions asked by salespeople. This shows that only the very best salespeople seem to be able to find the right questions.

Listening is not a natural thing. Research has shown that in conversation we will allow someone to speak, on average, for only 20 seconds before we interrupt them. Of this 20 seconds less than 5 seconds, on average, was listened to before thoughts of replying or contesting started. Think about the last time that you heard a friend telling a joke. The chances are that, fairly quickly, it reminded you of another joke. You may be aware that then your listening to their joke was diluted with, at best, partial attention. Often in this scenario people will rehearse their own joke in their head while the other person is still talking, with consequent lack of listening. They will miss the punch line! The same applies in selling.

Let us look at *Customer Agenda* questions. They can be broken into three groups:-

'Past' questions

These are questions about the facts of the existing situation. There is some evidence that in complex sales, lots of 'Fact' questions reduce success. A complex sale would take over 10 visits and more than one year to negotiate. In most sales, Present and Future questions are the most effective. Remember to take into account the behaviour model in Chapter 3. People behaving as Dominant Hostile or Dominant Warm will resist or dislike factual questions. With them you need to ask 'future' questions until they *bounce* the 'future' question.

Some examples of Past questions are:

- 'What products have you had'?
- 'How long have you had them'?

- 'Have you seen anything elsewhere that you like'?
- 'How has market condition affected you?'
- 'What have your competitors done?'
- 'Who have you bought these from in the past?'

'Present questions'

Present questions highlight existing concerns. I never talk about problems with a customer. A problem is a goal that cannot be attained. If you ask people, do they have any problems with their existing system?, you will miss out many things that concern them. For example 'Do you have any problems dealing with technical breakdowns in your other factory?' 'No' (they just get a helicopter to fly out a senior engineer when they have a problem). Compared with 'What concerns do you have dealing with people in your other factory?' Which question is more likely to highlight the need for video conferencing, faxes etc? Some sales teams keep a 'problem' box. You forfeit 20p every time you use the word.

Some other examples of Present questions:

- 'What do you like most about your existing product/situation/ supplier'?
- 'What changes are you currently making?'
- 'Where do you currently buy?'
- 'What is it about your current supplier that you like?'
- 'What is it about your current supplier that you dislike?'

Future Questions

At this stage salespeople normally jump in with a solution to the opportunity that has been created by the Present questions. In fact, there is still no stated desire to change this. We know that customers will take more action (*Consistency*) if they state a desire to change something. Without future questions what the salesperson is doing is leaving the customer to analyse the impact of the need on their own. If the customer decides the need is greater than the cost they will buy. The salesperson is leaving the decision to chance. More success can be obtained by getting the customer to turn that opportunity into a need. This is critical.

The biggest training deficit in salespeople I have experienced is not exploring the need. The biggest differentiator between the most successful salespeople and others is that successful salespeople work at changing opportunities into needs. Needs are all created from *future questions*.

What is a need question? Well it depends on the opportunity. Let's take the previous example: 'What concerns do you have about dealing with your other factory?' If this produced the response, 'Because of the distance involved a one hour meeting effectively takes a whole day', a 'need question' takes the opportunity into the future; e.g., 'What is the knock-on effect of that?' Answers may include: 'I don't have enough meetings and so performance suffers', 'I have to work harder than I should', 'I don't have enough time', 'I spend more time on the motorway than I would like to'. Instead of selling the customer a mobile phone, the clever salesperson would really tie this down by asking 'What would be the ideal solution for you?' The more needs the customer expresses the more successful you will be.

In any negotiation it is not the strength of the argument that wins the day but the number of arguments put forward. One great argument is not as good as ten good arguments. The salesperson may need to help the customer with the answer, prompting them to think along the right lines. The more needs expressed by the customer the more successful the salesperson. A need question therefore gets the customer to think of the future impact of the opportunity. What would be the impact of you not improving your selling skills? If the impact would be lower sales, lower commission, lower long-term success, lower self-esteem, fewer career opportunities, then it is worthwhile you continuing to read this book.

Opportunities are past, look for future needs

Other examples of how to change an opportunity into a need are:

- 'How does that fit with your long term goals?'
- 'What effect will that have on sales?'

- 'What would you expect to happen next?'
- 'What would you like to change about your current supplier/ service/product?'

Successful questioning techniques can be very easy, just ask about the past, the present and then the future. Of course it will be much more difficult than that because we have to listen to the answers and then think about what is not being said.

The real problem is that people don't ask direct questions. Let me give you an example. Your partner asks, 'Are you going into the kitchen?', is that a direct question? Do they want to know? Isn't it more likely that they want you to make tea? 'Have you got £20?' is more likely to mean, 'Will you lend me £20?'. 'Do you have a headache?' I will leave you to work that out for yourself... In fact it would be very boring if we only asked direct questions. Asking indirect questions helps people to develop rapport. When we share the meaning of an indirect question we have a greater sense of rapport. This can be seen with lovers who have a shared 'secret language'. Customers often make indirect statements, as we shall see when we look at addressing concerns.

A technique for preparing yourself to deal effectively with customers is to record all the questions they ask you for one month. You should then brainstorm with your colleagues what the real question is. Once you have this information you will then need to decide appropriate responses to the real question. I am sure you will find some startling results from this exercise.

You may find you have difficulty thinking of a good question to ask the customer and I have a brilliant method for thinking of the next question. It's called... *Listen to the last answer!* Imagine you asked me a question: 'Do you have any hobbies?, and I replied just three words 'I play golf'. If you listen to those three words, I don't know about you, but I can think of dozens of questions. 'Where do you play?', 'Who do you play with?', 'What do you like about golf?' 'What is your handicap?', etc. All you have to do is listen to the answer but we have already seen how difficult listening is.

Try this:

Say out loud the letters used in STOP.

Now, what do you do when you come to a green light?

If you are like millions of other people your brain switched off before you got to green light and had assumed I was going to ask about a red light. (We GO at green lights, by the way).

Remember the Rudyard Kipling poem as well:

> *I keep six honest serving men*
> *They taught me all I knew*
> *Their names are What and Why and When*
> *and How and Where and Who.*

This may help you to think of questions. One word of caution: 'Why?' is the most dangerous word in selling and it is also the most powerful. This is because of what happens in our brain when we are asked the question 'Why?'. It can be interpreted as interrogative and therefore may elicit a defensive response.

Think of this: imagine you were looking for a new car and you didn't want an estate model. If the salesperson asks: 'Why don't you want an estate?' you would give them all the reasons why – they are clunky, boring, etcetera. By doing this, we confirm to ourselves, and out loud to others, that we don't want an estate. This can only make it harder, because of people's need for *Consistency*, to sell an estate. But what if the salesman said: 'I wonder, what is it about estates that people don't like?', the customer might, just might, say something like, 'Well I do like lots of luggage space but I don't like everything being in full view and they are a bit slower (*unspoken*: besides, my neighbour drives a Volvo and I dislike him intensely...!).' The point is, avoiding asking 'Why?' might give you some good opportunities to sell to, rather than just a list of negatives. A better way still would be to chat to the customer about their lifestyle. If, for example, you found out about their family, their big dog, their need to carry around display material/tools/furniture, etc., then selling an Estate car may be both possible and professional. This discussion of the customer's lifestyle avoids them saying something they will find it hard to come back from and can lead on to more positive discussion of the positive merits of an estate, whatever they are.

There is another aspect to asking why? My wife said to me 'Can we pop in and see Sue and Richard on the way home?' When I automatically answered, 'Why?', she said, 'OK, it doesn't matter then'. I had no objection to popping in I just wondered if there were any specific reasons! (There's an example of that shorthand I mentioned between husband and wife causing mistrust!) If customers see 'Why?' questions as the same challenge then it is not a good way to find out what they are thinking or to develop rapport. 'How?' is better.

Just on a point of order, 'Why not?' is a loaded question too. The same rules apply as with 'Why?'. 'Why not?' can be successfully used to flag up a suggestion ('Why not try it for a month and see how you get on?'). But 'Why not?' by itself is a desperation question that shows you have lost. It is also bad manners. Why a customer does not choose to buy from you is none of your business! (Why he chooses not to buy from you is a different matter...) 'May I ask why not?' should only be used as a Past question, as in: 'Why did you decide not to do that?'.

There is a good place to ask 'Why?'. When a customer gives you a buying signal, say, 'I would prefer to buy from you'. If you ask 'Why?' in a non-threatening way, it makes it harder for them to back down again. To do this in a non-threatening way, try to hide the word why somewhere in the sentence. For example 'Oh that is very interesting, would you mind if I asked, why that is?'

Now, are you in a position to propose some solutions to the customer?

Summary

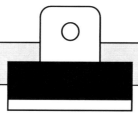

- **The Buying Process**

    - **Unaware of the Need**
    - **Aware of the Need**
    - **Analyse the Impact of the Need**
    - **Decide Response to the Need**
    - **Decide the Buying Criteria**
    - **Choose the Supplier**

- **Salesperson's Agenda questions destroy trust.**
  Customers Agenda questions build trust.

- **Listen to customers.**

- **Avoid asking 'Why?' when your hear an objection.**
  Always ask 'Why?' when you hear a buying signal

Newspaper Adverts...

- Illiterate? Write today for free help.

- Auto Repair Service. Free pick-up and delivery. Try us once, you'll never go anywhere again.

- Our experienced Mom will care for your child. Fenced yard, meals, and smacks included.

- Dog for sale: eats anything and is fond of children.

- Man wanted to work in dynamite factory. Must be willing to travel.

- Stock up and save. Limit: one.

- Semi-Annual after-Christmas Sale.

- 3-year old teacher needed for pre-school. Experience preferred.

- Mixing bowl set designed to please a cook with round bottom for efficient beating.

- Girl wanted to assist magician in cutting-off-head illusion.

- Dinner Special – Turkey $2.35; Chicken or Beef $2.25; Children $2.00

- For sale: antique desk suitable for lady with thick legs and large drawers.

- Now is your chance to have your cars pierced and get an extra pair to take home, too.

8

Propose Solutions

Before proposing solutions to customers let me explain the difference between **Persuading** and **Understanding**. This is quite difficult to do in a book so let me use what I do on training courses to illustrate this to delegates. I would urge you to try this out for yourself and see how effective a switch in thinking can be.

I find someone in the group that has a fear of water and I ask them if they would sit at the front. I then ask if anyone in the group loves sailing. I ask that person to persuade the volunteer that sailing is fun.

What happens as you can probably imagine is that the sailor uses lots of emotional language to indicate how much fun it is. Although as I have said Emotion is a very strong motivator the sailor is using their own Emotions. It is difficult to persuade using your own Emotions. There are two main things that usually come out of this exercise:-

- When we try to persuade we do most of the talking
- When this section is finished the person with the fear has almost invariably become more resistant to trying sailing!

The next thing I do is to ask the whole group to try to understand the fear. I have to consistently stop them from immediately going back to *persuading*. For example the volunteer often says they don't like being out of their depth. The group goes back to *persuading* and suggests the person try sailing in a swimming pool first of all. Two things also become clear when we change the direction from *persuading* to *understanding*.

- When we try to understand we do more listening.

- When we have understood, the volunteer is more receptive to our help.

It often happens that the volunteer still won't try sailing, that is not the point – some do, some don't. You can't sell to everyone. The point is that *understanding* increases our chances of selling ideas to people. Most agree to being more receptive to trying.

If I can understand what is stopping you from buying and tailor my solutions taking these into account I MUST be more successful!

You are now in the situation that you have all the information necessary in which to propose a solution. From now on, the going becomes more dangerous. Up until now you have been helping the customer to give you information. Everything has been non-threatening and you have built up enormous trust with the customer. If you abuse the trust they will never forgive you. This is where the test of openness and honesty comes in.

In my experience, salespeople seem to find it hard to stick rigidly to the truth about what they will do. Even excluding unforeseen circumstances that prevent them from doing what they say they will do. There was a study in the Times recently (which I think is a gross exaggeration, incidentally) that the average human tells 200 lies per day. Maybe it is harder to tell the truth!

With regard to product performance it is hard to inform customers that the products sometimes go wrong whilst maintaining the delicate balance of retaining confidence and selling your product.

Any solution that you propose will have good points and bad points and it makes sense to think of both. It may seem strange, but I am in favour of telling the customer as much as possible about your proposed solutions. I advocate even telling them what you see as being negative.

The reason for this is quite clear to me:-

I should at least be able to put a case for buying that sounds logical to me; i.e., that the positives outweigh the negatives.

This does not mean I am saying that everyone should buy for the same reasons as me – far from it. I am saying that if they buy for the same reasons as me then they will buy the logic of my reasons for buying. If they do not buy for the same reasons as me, and most people don't, then I will not put them off by telling them my perceived 'bad bits'. For example, if I am proposing a computer purchase, giving the good points and the bad points of two computers will build trust. It also helps the person to make the best decision for them. Basic honesty builds trust. Please also consider this in conjunction with the behaviour model. Some people really don't want your opinion anyway and you should stick to facts only with them.

Features and Benefits

So should you tell people about Features or Benefits? A feature is what a product is or has, or has on top of the basic spec., and a benefit is what it *does* for the customer. Conventional wisdom says people don't buy features, they buy benefits (this sounds logical but tell that to a teenager looking for a sound system!). Many trainers have also made it more complicated by introducing 'Features, Advantages and Benefits'. Well, as usual, I look at it in a practical way. It is logical that people buy benefits but we already know that buying decisions are made on an emotional basis. Features, Advantages and Benefits probably does add something but for me it is a complication that I can do without.

Most sales training concentrates on people buying 'benefits' not 'features'. If that is the case why would anyone buy a 9-band graphic equaliser on a hi-fi and not have a clue what it does? Why would people living in central London buy an off-road vehicle, or a person in East Anglia buy a mountain bike? How about a video recorder with a 14-day timer that nobody can use? I have heard that all Japanese technology today is going into developing a video recorder with a 14-day timer that even grownups can use. And what about the 199 numbers pre-set feature on your mobile phone, do you even know 199 people? Can you be bothered programming them all in? Have you figured out how? But you'd prefer it over the one with only 99...

I don't believe for one minute people buy benefits rather than features. Imagine, two products are advertised at the same price and one has more features than the other. Many people, not all, will buy the product with more features because of the perceived higher value. Look at a Personal Computer offer. This much clock speed, this much RAM... Free printer. Not a mention of benefits! I think you have to separate out the people who want bells and whistles (for me, Dominant and Submissive Warm people) and those who don't (Dominant and Submissive Hostile). I also think this is related to people who *move towards*, that want lots of features, and people who *move away* (more features means more complicated and more chance of breaking down). (For Moving Towards and Moving Away, see page 124.)

What tends to confuse this issue of Features or Benefits is that most customers want the features explained to them in a way that they can understand. For example, at the time of buying I would prefer a salesperson not to talk about the jargon of a 'graphic equaliser' or a 'woofer' or 'tweeter' to me and instead explain why they are better. In my experience they don't because they either don't know themselves (most common) or they can't put it into plain language.

So what about features? If I mention more benefits and less features will that add to my success? Well, let me tell you that salespeople who mention more features will be more successful. In fact, in my research successful sales have 3 times more features mentioned than failed sales. That is purely features; i.e., the feature was mentioned on its own with no associated benefit mentioned. Why is this? I think there are a few reasons.

Salespeople who mention more features are seen as being more knowledgeable about their product and we prefer to buy from people who are more knowledgeable.

You can divide features into three categories:-

● Standard; i.e., everybody has them (e.g., 4 wheels on a car.)

●

Company; i.e., associated with the size of the company, the brand, the length of time in business, the guarantee and a strong company to back it up.

● Differentiators – or, non-standard features that differentiate your product in the market place; i.e., your unique selling points; (e.g., Volvo has made safety one of its differentiators.)

Note that whether the feature is actually a differentiator is not the point. You can chose to make any feature a differentiator and build your brand on these features. The strength of the brand will only depend on how unique and how important customers see that feature as being.

For example, a car manufacturer may choose safety as their differentiator even when other manufacturers mostly have the same safety features. The determining factor is, can you convince others they are differentiators?

I would suggest that customers find it patronising to be told the benefits of standard features. This car has a 2-litre engine 'which means that you will get all the power you are looking for!' Don't tell me what I am looking for.

It is particularly important when giving your opinion to try and back it up with some evidence, such as a feature.

When it comes to benefits a different pattern emerges. Salespeople who mentioned more benefits actually had less success! Let me explain what I think happened. Part of the explanation is contained in the features; i.e., some benefits that were mentioned made the customer feel patronised. Some benefits were mentioned that didn't actually relate to the feature the salesperson was tying them to; e.g., in the 2-litre engine example above it does not necessarily follow that

123

a 2-litre engine is more *powerful* than a 1.6-litre (look at racing cars for confirmation). Also, some benefits were mentioned that didn't apply to that customer. (Maybe the customer didn't prefer power over good fuel economy?) This gave a signal that the salesperson hadn't listened to the customer's needs.

There was a consistent pattern with benefits. When a salesperson linked more benefits directly to the previously stated needs of the customer, in this case there was a direct correlation between the number of these 'specifically needed benefits' and success. More specifically needed benefits created more success. It is clear the successful salesperson is better at getting customers to express their needs and then linking their proposed solutions back to these expressed needs.

I have worked with a few organisations that seemed to understand this and have still missed the point. I have been asked to train people to mention only the benefits of previously stated needs. This ignores that the salesperson must be good at getting the customer to express the needs first of all. If you want to practise, then mention as many features and benefits as possible. Then observe which ones people seem more interested in. Then improve your questioning to find out which customers need which benefits. Only then should you reduce the number of benefits you propose by linking the benefits to their needs. Don't reduce the number of benefits you mention until you increase the number of needs you identify. I am constantly disappointed, in both retail and wholesale selling; by how little the product is talked about and how much time is spent talking about the 'deal', etcetera.

Moving towards and moving away

The entire world is full of only two types of people!! There are people who **'move towards'** and people who **'move away'**. It is rather like saying whether a glass is half full or half empty. They can be identified while you are identifying their needs. People will either tend to point out things that they like about the product (people who *move towards*) or in the main they will point out what they don't like about the product (people who *move away*).

Once identified it is important to recognise that people who *move towards* will prefer products that are new and innovative. Words used such as: -

- New
- Increase
- Exclusive
- Improved
- Trial offer
- Gain

...will appeal to these people. People who *move away* will prefer products that are guaranteed and safe. Words used in presentations such as: -

- Guaranteed
- Save
- Brand name
- Reduced
- Most popular
- As seen on TV

...will appeal more to these people.

People who *move towards* generally will not think about the possibility of a product breaking down. If too much is made of a guarantee they will begin to question the reliability of the product. With people who *move towards*, only use the guarantee as evidence of better quality; i.e,. to compare two items with different guarantee periods. If the guarantee is an industry standard, talk about the quality of the product not the guarantee. Most people *move towards*. The small numbers of people who complete guarantee cards are evidence of this. Manufacturers have now resorted to giving rewards (prize draws, etc.) to encourage people to fill in their guarantee cards.

It is also possible that we *move towards* when buying, say, a television (because we perceive most of them nowadays to be good quality) and *move away* when buying something we have had a bad experience with in the past; (e.g. I now *move away* with computers – thank you, Bill Gates!)

The following example illustrates the importance of linking your proposed solutions to the specific needs of the Customer:

A person has been trying to sell their home without success. They have decided to withdraw the property from the marketplace in the short term. They wish to improve the property with the view of selling the house in the future. The person *moves towards*, and they will not be interested in the most popular product.

Your proposed solution, however, is the most popular product. If you don't link it directly to their specific needs, it will not appeal to them. But which is the greater need? For your product, or to sell their house? The reason behind your suggestion is that the product is necessary to a successful outcome; i.e., that the most popular product would have the widest appeal for future potential home buyers. Despite this being a person that *moves towards*, it would appeal to them as a product that will appeal to others whom they wish to influence.

Throughout the sale you will increase your success ratio if you involve people by getting them to touch things, try things, turn them on and off, etc.

Selling add-ons

When you are selling add-ons the timing is critical to the success. Add-ons can be classified as **Enhancers** or **Protectors**. An *Enhancer* is something that enhances the ownership experience of the product; e.g., a CD player in a car. A *Protector* is something that protects the investment; e.g., Extended Warranty.

You must sell *Enhancers* during the sale and *Protectors* after the sale has been agreed. For instance, wine enhances a meal and so the waiter cannot sell it to you when you are leaving and just about to pay the bill. Alka Seltzer is a protector, you cannot sell it during a meal or the customer will think twice about eating in your restaurant!

Enhancer   Protector

Cheap or just inexpensive?

Be careful with the word 'cheap' when proposing solutions to customers. Cheap implies low quality and you should only use it when you intend to show that something is of lower quality. For example, if you are talking to a customer about the good quality of a product they are interested in. To show how it differs from another you could show them the differences between this and a cheaper product. Never talk about your own products as cheap, they are better value and less expensive but not cheap.

Finally remember, (Chapter 3 – Psychological Needs) when proposing solutions people have a need to *Visualise* themselves owning a product. Never forget the *Infectiousness of Enthusiasm*. You can ask questions which help people to *Visualise* owning the product such as asking them about how they will use the product in the future. The way you talk to them and the words you use will reflect your *Enthusiasm* for the product.

Summary

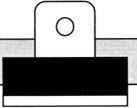

- *Understanding is more effective than Persuading.*

- *Make a case for buying that sounds logical to you.*

- *Words to use with people who 'Move Towards' are: -*

New	*Exclusive*	*Trial Offer*
Increase	*Improve*	*Gain*

  People who 'Move Away' will prefer: -

Guaranteed	*Brand Name*	*Most Popular*
Save	*Reduce*	*As seen on TV*

- *Features sell more than benefits as long as these are understood.*

- *Benefits must be linked to the specific needs of the buyer.*

- *Explain all features in language that the customers understands.*

- *Sell Enhancers during the sale*

  Sell Protectors after the sale

More Newspaper Adverts

- We do not tear your clothing with machinery. We do it carefully by hand.

- For sale. Three canaries of undermined sex.

- Great Dames for sale.

- Have several very old dresses from grandmother in beautiful condition.

- Vacation Special: have your home exterminated.

- Get rid of aunts. Zap does the job in 24 hours.

- Toaster: A gift that every member of the family appreciates. Automatically burns toast.

- For Rent: 6-room hated apartment.

- Man, honest. Will take anything.

- Used Cars: Why go elsewhere to be cheated. Come here first.

- Christmas tag-sale. Handmade gifts for the hard-to-find person.

- Wanted: Hair cutter. Excellent growth potential.

- Wanted. Widower with school age children requires person to assume general housekeeping duties. Must be capable of contributing to growth of family.

- The Superstore – unequalled in size, unmatched in variety, unrivalled inconvenience. *(Bet you know a few of those!)*

9

Addressing Concerns

You may presently consider addressing concerns as objection handling. If you use my strategy for addressing concerns you will get evidence they are only concerns by the number of people that handle them for themselves.

I think every salesperson has an answer to every concern of the customer. They can say why their product is a little more expensive than down the road. They know why this is better quality, etc. What they need is a way of getting the customer to listen to them and accept what they are saying! For this reason I have a process which increases the chances of getting the customer to listen to your answer.

Addressing concerns is another opportunity to undo all the good work you have done to build up trust with the customer. Customers expect a salesman to argue with them when they express concerns or objections. If you do that at any time then trust goes out of the window. Stop arguing and start empathising.

One difficulty when addressing concerns is that, as we have seen in Chapter 7 – Questioning Techniques, people don't always ask the real question. They don't always – or even often – voice the real concern.

Preferred responses

Fundamental to addressing concerns is the concept of **Preferred Responses**. If someone asks 'Do you want a cup of tea?', the *Preferred Response* is 'Yes, please' and people can give that response without any further explanation. If the response is 'No, thank you' people will feel the need to explain. For example people say 'No thank you I've just had one' or, 'I am in a hurry' or, 'I don't drink tea' etc.

This is because they are giving a *non-Preferred Response* and they feel the need to explain. This concept can be used to great effect in addressing concerns.

You have probably never heard it in your business, but imagine a customer saying to you:-

'That's too Expensive'

What are the different things the customer could mean by that phrase? I can think of the following:

- I can't afford it.
- I can afford it but it is more than I want to spend.
- I can afford it but it is more than I thought it would be.
- Is there any way you can give me a discount?
- It is less expensive elsewhere.
- I can't see any difference between that one and this one that is cheaper.

I would argue that each of these concerns would have to be handled a different way. In my experience salespeople continually respond too quickly to statements such as 'That's too expensive'.

Because this is a *non-Preferred Response* I suggest you build in to your selling style a slight pause anytime you hear what you think is an objection or a concern. I promise you people will add an explanation to their comment and the second thing they say is the real concern.

You will also find when you leave a pause a surprising number of people will address their own concern. For example 'That's too expensive (pause) I can't see how that can be more expensive than this but hold on, this one does have the gold finish'.

Try it. I guarantee it works.

The next thing you need to do to avoid argument is to empathise with the customer. Let's assume you get the concern: 'I need to think about it'. (Incidentally if you do get this concern I think you have caused it, as I will explain in the next chapter (10 – Agreeing Future Action).

The average salesperson says something like, 'I understand that but what is it you want to think about'. This is not empathy. The use of the word 'but' is critical here. Have you ever had someone say to you 'I understand how you feel, but....'? That means they don't understand at all. 'Yes, but...' means no! I agree completely, but! To the listener it means I don't agree at all.

When addressing concerns it is really important not to use the word 'but'; or any variation of it, such as 'however', 'on the other hand', etc. Many languages other than English have two words for our 'but'. One that means 'but', and one that means 'and also'. Sadly, we have only one. The use of 'but' is perfectly acceptable when we want to show that the first part of the sentence is less important. For example 'I used to lack confidence when selling 'but' now I feel more confident. If you use 'and' it may seem awkward to you, and you will find you can add something to what people are saying. This is preferable to saying that the first part of your sentence is unimportant. It is the difference between saying 'I understand how you feel but why don't you look at it this way?', and: 'I understand how you feel and if I could give you some more information would that help you?'

People who say 'they need to think about it' sometimes aren't giving the real concern. This could be either:

- I want to get out
- I need to think about it.

I want to get out

Put yourself in their place and empathise with them. 'I understand completely and it is a big decision. I wouldn't want you to make a mistake either. The average buyer of our products uses them for 15 years and you wouldn't want to live for the next fifteen years regretting your decision. Let's just go through everything thoroughly to make sure everything is right for you'.

I need to think about it

I often find myself in the situation where it is completely understandable for the customer to go away and think about it. In this case I use their need to reciprocate in order to increase the chances of them coming back. In order to do this I could:-

- Give them my 'office copy' of the manual they were looking at.
- Make an appointment for them.
- Arrange to alter the product they were looking at to how exactly it would look if we fitted the accessory kit, etc.
- Arrange to collect them.

In short, do anything that is specifically *for them*. Because of the need to reciprocate, if people have no intention of coming back they will let you know now.

When you have addressed all concerns you must now do what every successful salesperson I have ever met does consistently and always does it at the same stage. They agree future action.

Summary

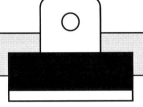

- *Preferred Responses mean that people will want to give you an explanation.*

- *Empathise with the customer.*

- *Use Reciprocation when people need time to think it over.*

- *Avoid arguing.*

- *Don't use 'But', However', 'Although' – conditional conjunctions. Instead, use 'And'.*

"Dear Technical Support..."

I'm currently running the latest version of GirlFriend and I've been having some problems lately. I've been running the same version of DrinkingBuddies 1.0 forever as my primary application, and all the GirlFriend releases I've tried have always conflicted with it. I hear that DrinkingBuddies won't crash if GirlFriend is run in background mode and the sound is turned off. But I'm embarrassed to say I can't find the switch to turn the sound off. I just run them separately, and it works okay.

GirlFriend also seems to have a problem co-existing with my Golf program, often trying to abort Golf with some sort of timing incompatibility. I probably should have stayed with GirlFriend 1.0, but I thought I might see better performance from GirlFriend 2.0. After months of conflicts and other problems, I consulted a friend who has had experience with GirlFriend 2.0. He said I probably didn't have enough cache to run GirlFriend 2.0, and eventually it would require a Token Ring to run properly. He was right, as soon as I purged my cache it uninstalled itself. Shortly after that, I installed GirlFriend 3.0 beta. All the bugs were supposed to be gone, but the first time I used it, it gave me a virus anyway. I had to clean out my whole system and shut down for a while.

I very cautiously upgraded to GirlFriend 4.0. This time I used a SCSI probe first and also installed a virus protection program. It worked okay for a while until I discovered that GirlFriend 1.0 was still in my system. I tried running GirlFriend 1.0 again with GirlFriend 4.0 still installed, but GirlFriend 4.0 has a feature I didn't know about that automatically senses the presence of any other version of GirlFriend and communicates with it in some way, which results in the immediate removal of both versions. The version I have now works pretty well, but there are still some problems. Like all versions of GirlFriend, it is written in some obscure language I can't understand, much less reprogram. Frankly I think there is too much attention paid to the look and feel rather than the desired functionality. Also, to get the best connections with your hardware, you usually have to use gold-plated contacts. And I've never liked how GirlFriend is totally 'object-oriented.'

A year ago, a friend of mine upgraded his version of GirlFriend to GirlFriendPlus 1.0, which is a Terminate and Stay Resident version of GirlFriend. He discovered that GirlFriendPlus 1.0 expires within a year if you don't upgrade to Fiancee 1.0. So he did, but soon after that, he had to upgrade to Wife 1.0, which he describes as a huge resource hog. It has taken up all his space, so he can't load anything else. One of the primary reasons he decided to go with Wife 1.0 was because it came bundled with FreeSexPlus. Well, it turns out the resource allocation module of Wife 1.0 sometimes prohibits access to FreeSexPlus, particularly the new Plug-Ins he wanted to try. On top of that, Wife 1.0 must be running on a well warmed-up system before he can do anything.

Although he did not ask for it, Wife 1.0 came with MotherInLaw module which has an automatic pop-up feature he can't turn off. I told him to try installing Mistress 1.0, but he said he heard if you try to run it without first uninstalling Wife 1.0, Wife 1.0 will delete MSMoney files before doing the uninstall itself. Then Mistress 1.0 won't install anyway because of insufficient resources. Any Ideas???

10

Agree Future Action

When I run training courses I ask delegates what they would like to work on. Many of them say closing skills. It is better to improve their selling before they try to close rather than selling poorly and improving their closing skills. If you do a poor job selling you have not earned the right to close.(This chapter is only as good as the actions you have taken prior to getting to this stage.)

Having said that, the easiest decision for people to make is not to make a decision. Successful salespeople always have strategies to help people to make a decision. Further, they always use these strategies in order to agree some form of future action with the customer. If you don't ask customers to commit to some future action then many won't take any action at all, or will take it with salespeople who *have* asked for a commitment.

In this entire book I believe you can do anything I have mentioned as often as you like, and you could be the best salesperson ever. You can do anything I have said, in any order – but if you don't agree future action at the right time you will not be as successful as you should be.

You can never learn the right way to agree future action by doing it too late or asking for too little action. You can only learn the right way by asking for too much and asking too quickly. Customers never tell you when you were too late and asked for too little. Try asking for commitment as early as possible until you get it right.

It is a good strategy in business-to-business selling to organise your next meeting at the current meeting, no matter how far in the future that may be. It is easier to move a meeting than it is to arrange one. Meetings that are arranged have a higher chance of happening than meetings that haven't been arranged at all...

One of the techniques I have used for getting customers to agree future action is asking them what they think. If you do this often enough you will never get the concern, 'I need to think about it'. I have found one of the hardest things to get around is when a customer has said, 'I need to think about it'. I find it really hard to get them to do so in front of me. I realised I was causing the concern by not allowing them to think about it throughout the process. The more I said to them, during the sale, 'What do you think about that?', the less they said they needed to think about it at the end.

When I ask: 'What do you think about that?' near the end, it is amazing how many people will offer future action by asking: 'How quickly can we have it?'. I have found this to be an 'instant gratification' society. When people have said to me they are in no hurry, if I say, 'I can get it here for Wednesday for you, would that be soon enough?' I find lots of people saying yes. 'I have only one left in stock, is that enough for you?'. I was taught this as the 'enough' close.

I think most of the 'traditional' closes are no longer as successful and my preferred close is to agree future action by asking if people want to go ahead or want to go to the next stage etc.

Discounting

If you do think you have to give a discount; and personally, I don't think any business needs to (I can hear the *Yeah/Buts* again), here are some rules that you may want to try when you think it is appropriate to offer one. These rules reduce the risk of offering a discount and still not getting a sale.

- Make sure the customer knows the product is worth the original value. You do this by sticking to the original price at least three times.
- There must be a good reason for the discount.
- It should include an *inconvenience* to the customer.

Examples of good reasons and inconveniences are:

- If the customer takes early delivery or pays in full it may allow you to place your next order with the manufacturers during their discount period or sale.
- You may also consider not giving a reduction in the price and look at giving goods to the value of the discount and improve stock turn.

By the way, some interesting research on discounts:-

- Customers are suspicious of 'round figures'; e.g., 10 per cent, £100, etc.
- Customers are suspicious of a high starting point; e.g., 50 per cent off.
- Customers are suspicious of large jumps. An increase in discount from 10 per cent to 15 per cent represents a 50 per cent jump in the discount.
- The longer the calculation and the more documents referred to during the calculation the more accurate the discount is perceived to be. People are less likely to keep going for more.

If you give a 10 per cent discount at the moment how much business would you lose if you cut it to 9 per cent tomorrow? If the answer is 'none', then do it. Then next month how much would you lose if you reduced it to 8 per cent? Again, if 'none', then do it and keep doing it until you find out the level you need to discount to avoid losing business. This is called the **Just Noticeable Difference**.

Supermarkets use the *Just Noticeable Difference* to find out how much they need to discount to increase the sale of an item; e.g., If they discount beans by 1p do the sales increase? If not, how about 2p. They keep going until they find out.(In the great Baked Bean war of the mid-'90s, they ended up paying customers to take them away!)

Summary

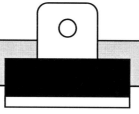

- *Always Agree Future Action.*
- *Rules for discounting:*
    - *Make it worth the original value.*
    - *There must be a good reason for the discount.*
    - *It should be an inconvenience to the customer.*
    - *Avoid round figures.*
    - *Avoid a high starting point.*
    - *Avoid large jumps.*
    - *Use a calculator, make it a long calculation and refer to lots of price lists.*
- *Continually test how much you need to give in discount; find your 'Just Noticeable Difference'.*

11

Follow-up

By now I am sure you will be surprised to read that I am different with regard to follow-up! I am sure most people have more effective follow-up systems than I do. Here are my thoughts:-

Most salespeople seem to ask at some time why they didn't get business? Very few seem to do anything about the information they receive. I have never followed-up any business I didn't get. I see it as a waste of time better spent taking steps to get the next sale. That is not to say that 'lost' sales cannot occasionally be rescued. I feel that the amount of effort put in for the meagre return is inefficient.

Very few salespeople seem to ask why they did get business and that is far more important to me. I always ask why clients chose me in preference to competitors. In accordance with my style, I focus on playing to my strengths.

Many successful salespeople have a systemised referral process and I am sure it works for them. I haven't, and prefer to rely on making unconditional contact with people. I get as many referrals as I would like and if this system dries up then I will look to implement a referral process. I would recommend a system if I could find one that doesn't seem to me to be an abuse of a valued relationship. If clients want to recommend me to others I am sure they will do it without me asking. I find it uncomfortable using a referral process with clients and I am uncomfortable when friends ask me to recommend them. I realise this is my own 'comfort zone' and it is a conscious decision.

I would like to make unconditional contact with any reader about their thoughts on this and any other issues I have raised. Please feel free to e-mail me at <u>david@gtiuk.com</u>

I would wish you luck if I believed luck had anything to do with being successful. The application of the principles in this book will have a far greater impact on your success than luck ever could. Have fun and enjoy the journey.

Solutions

The solution to the algebra on page 14 lies in dividing at the end by $(a^2 - ab)$. Because $a = b$, then $(a^2 - ab)$ is equal to zero. When you divide a number by zero you get infinity. (Another way of putting it is: you can't divide a number by zero at all, so it's not really a valid parameter). Either way, it does not follow that because 1x0 is the same as 2x0, then 1 is the same as 2.

Restaurant conundrum (page 24): How £30 is only £29... It's a trick! The £2 in the waiter's pocket has come out of the £10 each has paid and is not in addition to it. Add the £2 tip to the £25 left in the till and you have £27... Add each pound the 3 diners have and you get £30.

The solution to Prison Problem on page 58 is that the man in the middle thinks to himself, 'If the man behind me could see two hats the same colour he would know the colour of his own hat. Because he isn't saying anything then he must see one white hat and one black hat and, since I can see a white hat, my own hat must be black'.

Concepts